At Sylvan, we believe reading is one of life's most important, most personal, most meaningful skills, and we're so glad you've taken this step to become a successful reader with us. We know spelling is a critical process that mirrors and complements the reading process. Third-grade spellers are learning to spell more intricate patterns and longer words. A strong foundation in spelling prepares third-graders to spell more challenging words in upcoming grades and makes them stronger readers.

At Sylvan, successful spelling instruction encompasses numerous spelling processes with research-based, developmentally appropriate, and highly motivating, entertaining, and thought-provoking lessons. The learning process relies on high standards and meaningful parental involvement. With success, students feel increasing confidence. With increasing confidence, students build even more success. It's a perfect cycle. That's why our Sylvan workbooks aren't like the others. We're laying out the roadmap for learning. The rest is in your hands.

Parents, you have a special role. While your child is working, stay within earshot. If he needs help or gets stuck, you can be there to get him on the right track. And you're always there with supportive encouragement and plenty of celebratory congratulations.

One of the best ways to master spelling is to check one's own work. Often the answer is just a dictionary away, so that's always a good place to start. Each section of the workbook also includes a Check It! strip. As your child completes the activities, he can check his answers with Check It! If he sees any errors, he can fix them himself.

At Sylvan, our goal is confident spellers who have the skills to tackle anything they want to read. We love learning. We want all children to love it as well.

Included with your purchase is a coupon for a discount on our in-center service. As your child continues on his academic journey, your local Sylvan Learning Center can partner with your family in ensuring your child remains a confident, successful, and independent learner.

The Sylvan Team

D1122264

Sylvan Learning Center.
Unleash your child's potential here.

No matter how big or small the academic challenge, every child has the ability to learn. But sometimes children need help making it happen. Sylvan believes every child has the potential to do great things. And, we know better than anyone else how to tap into that academic potential so that a child's future really is full of possibilities. Sylvan Learning Center is the place where your child can build and master the learning skills needed to succeed and unlock the potential you know is there.

The proven, personalized approach of our in-center programs deliver unparalleled results that other supplemental education services simply can't match. Your child's achievements will be seen not only in test scores and report cards but outside the classroom as well. And when he starts achieving his full potential, everyone will know it. You will see a new level of confidence come through in everything he does and every interaction he has.

How can Sylvan's personalized in-center approach help your child unleash his potential?

- Starting with our exclusive Sylvan Skills Assessment®, we pinpoint your child's exact academic needs.

- Then we develop a customized learning plan designed to achieve your child's academic goals.

- Through our method of skill mastery, your child will not only learn and master every skill in his personalized plan, he will be truly motivated and inspired to achieve his full potential.

To get started, included with this Sylvan product purchase is $10 off our exclusive Sylvan Skills Assessment®. Simply use this coupon and contact your local Sylvan Learning Center to set up your appointment.

And to learn more about Sylvan and our innovative in-center programs, call 1-800-EDUCATE or visit www.educate.com. *With over 1,000 locations in North America, there is a Sylvan Learning Center near you!*

3rd-Grade Spelling Success

Published in the United States by Random House, Inc., New York, and in Canada by Random
House of Canada Limited, Toronto.

www.tutoring.sylvanlearning.com

Created by Smarterville Productions LLC
Cover and Interior Photos: Jonathan Pozniak
Cover and Interior Illustrations: Duendes del Sur

First Edition

ISBN: 978-0-375-43001-5

Library of Congress Cataloging-in-Publication Data available upon request.

This book is available at special discounts for bulk purchases for sales promotions or premiums.
For more information, write to Special Markets/Premium Sales, 1745 Broadway, MD 6-2,
New York, New York 10019 or e-mail specialmarkets@randomhouse.com.

PRINTED IN CHINA

10 9 8 7 6 5 4 3 2 1

Contents

Checking your answers is part of the learning.

Each section of the workbook begins with an easy-to-use Check It! strip.

1. Before beginning the activities, cut out the Check It! strip.

2. As you complete the activities on each page, check your answers.

3. If you find an error, you can correct it yourself.

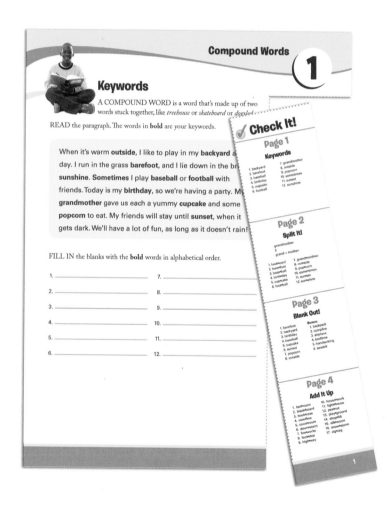

Keywords

A COMPOUND WORD is a word that's made up of two words stuck together, like *treehouse* or *skateboard* or *dogsled*.

READ the paragraph. The words in **bold** are your keywords.

When it's warm **outside**, I like to play in my **backyard** all day. I run in the grass **barefoot**, and I lie down in the bright **sunshine**. **Sometimes** I play **baseball** or **football** with friends. Today is my **birthday**, so we're having a party. My **grandmother** gave us each a yummy **cupcake** and some **popcorn** to eat. My friends will stay until **sunset**, when it gets dark. We'll have a lot of fun, as long as it doesn't rain!

FILL IN the blanks with the **bold** words in alphabetical order.

1. _____
2. _____
3. _____
4. _____
5. _____
6. _____
7. _____
8. _____
9. _____
10. _____
11. _____
12. _____

Check It!

Page 1

Keywords

1. backyard
2. barefoot
3. baseball
4. birthday
5. cupcake
6. football
7. grandmother
8. outside
9. popcorn
10. sometimes
11. sunset
12. sunshine

Page 2

Split It!

grandmother
3
grand + mother

1. back•yard
2. bare•foot
3. base•ball
4. birth•day
5. cup•cake
6. foot•ball
7. grand•moth•er
8. out•side
9. pop•corn
10. some•times
11. sun•set
12. sun•shine

Page 3

Blank Out!

1. barefoot
2. backyard
3. birthday
4. baseball
5. cupcake
6. sunset
7. popcorn
8. outside

Bonus:
1. backpack
2. campfire
3. airplane
4. bedtime
5. handwriting
6. seasick

Page 4

Add It Up

1. bed•room
2. black•board
3. book•case
4. care•free
5. court•room
6. down•stairs
7. fire•works
8. foot•step
9. high•way
10. house•work
11. light•house
12. pea•nut
13. play•ground
14. shop•lift
15. silk•worm
16. snow•storm
17. zig•zag

Split It!

Which one of the keywords has more than two syllables?

grandmother

How many syllables does it have? *3*

Break it down: What two smaller words make up the bigger word?

grand + *mother*

When you split a compound word into syllables, start by breaking it down into the smaller words and putting a dot in between the words. Then, if one of the words has more than one syllable (like *mother*), put a dot between the syllables.

SPLIT the keywords into syllables, using dots to mark the breaks.

Examples: skate•board, step•fa•ther

backyard	1.	*back•yard*
barefoot	2.	*bare•foot* foot
baseball	3.	*base•ball*
birthday	4.	*birth•day*
cupcake	5.	*cup•cake*
football	6.	*foot•ball* ball
grandmother	7.	*grand•moth•er*
outside	8.	*out•side*
popcorn	9.	*pop•corn* corn
sometimes	10.	*some•times*
sunset	11.	*sun•set*
sunshine	12.	*sun•shine*

Blank Out!

FILL IN the blanks with keywords.

1. Without shoes or socks, your *foot* is *bare*.

   You are _*barefoot*_.

2. The grassy *yard* in the *back* of our house is the _*backyard*_.

3. Every year you celebrate the *day* of your *birth*. Happy _*birthday*_ !

4. If you hit a *ball* and run to a *base*, you're playing _*baseball*_.

5. A small *cake* shaped like a *cup* is a _*cupcake*_.

6. After the *sun* has *set*, it's dark outside. Be home by _*sunset*_ !

7. If you heat up a kernel of *corn*, it will *pop*. That's called _*popcorn*_.

8. When you go *out* the front or back *side* of your house, you're _*outside*_.

Bonus

Can you finish these sentences?

1. A *pack* that you fill with books and carry on your *back* is a _*backpack*_

2. When you *camp* in a tent and roast marshmallows over a *fire*,

   that's a _*campfire*_

3. A *plane* that flies through the *air* from New York to London is an _*airplane*_.

4. At night, when the clock says it's *time* to go to *bed*, it's _*bedtime*_ .

5. The words you are *writing* with your pen in your *hand* is _*handwriting*_

6. If sailing on the *sea* makes you so *sick* you

   throw up, you're _*seasick*_ .

Compound Words

Add It Up

ADD UP the smaller words to make compound words.
SPLIT the new words into syllables. FILL IN the blanks, using dots to mark the breaks.

Example: skate + board = skate•board

bed	+ room	=	1.	*bed•room*
black	+ board	=	2.	*black•board*
book	+ case	=	3.	*book•case*
care	+ free	=	4.	*care•free*
court	+ room	=	5.	*court•room*
down	+ stairs	=	6.	*down•stairs*
fire	+ works	=	7.	*fire•works*
foot	+ step	=	8.	*foot•step*
high	+ way	=	9.	*high•way*
house	+ work	=	10.	*house•work*
light	+ house	=	11.	*light•house*
pea	+ nut	=	12.	*pea•nut*
play	+ ground	=	13.	*play•ground*
shop	+ lift	=	14.	*shop•lift*
silk	+ worm	=	15.	*shop•lift*
snow	+ storm	=	16.	*snow•storm*
zig	+ zag	=	17.	*zig•zag*

✓ Check It!

Cut out the Check It! section on page 1, and see if you got the answers right.

Keywords

Two-syllable words with a DOUBLE CONSONANT in the middle (like *middle*) are easy to split into syllables. The dot goes between the double letters, just like this: mid•dle.

READ the paragraph. The words in **bold** are your keywords.

After **soccer** practice last week, I was in a **hurry**. Mom would **worry** and **holler** at me if I got home late. It was a **rotten**, rainy day. I was cold and grumpy. In my rush, I almost fell over a **kitten** in a **shallow puddle**! I picked her up so I could **carry** her home. I dried her off and tied a **ribbon** around her neck. She fell asleep on my **pillow**. Now she will **follow** me everywhere!

FILL IN the blanks with the **bold** words in alphabetical order.

1. _____
2. _____
3. _____
4. _____
5. _____
6. _____

7. _____
8. _____
9. _____
10. _____
11. _____
12. _____

 **Check It!**

Page 5

Keywords

1. carry	7. puddle
2. follow	8. ribbon
3. holler	9. rotten
4. hurry	10. shallow
5. kitten	11. soccer
6. pillow	12. worry

Page 6

Split It!

1. car•ry	7. pud•dle
2. fol•low	8. rib•bon
3. hol•ler	9. rot•ten
4. hur•ry	10. shal•low
5. kit•ten	11. soc•cer
6. pil•low	12. wor•ry

Page 7

Blank Out!

1. kitten	5. worry
2. carry	6. rotten
3. follow	7. holler
4. hurry	

Mix & Match

1. attack	6. possess
2. banner	7. pollute
3. collect	8. tunnel
4. current	9. yellow
5. million	10. scatter

Page 8

Spotlight

Consonants: b, c, d, f, g, h, j, k, l, m, n, p, q, r, s, t, v, w, x, y, z
Vowels: a, e, i, o, u (sometimes y)

Split It!

Double Consonants	Double Vowels
1. hobby	1. aardvark
2. lasso	2. creepy
3. merry	3. needle
4. sputter	4. scooper
5. upper	5. skiing

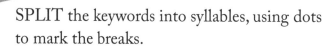

Split It!

SPLIT the keywords into syllables, using dots to mark the breaks.

HINT: Remember, the split happens between the double letters.

Example: middle   mid•dle

carry	1. _____
follow	2. _____
holler	3. _____
hurry	4. _____
kitten	5. _____
pillow	6. _____
puddle	7. _____
ribbon	8. _____
rotten	9. _____
shallow	10. _____
soccer	11. _____
worry	12. _____

Blank Out!

FILL IN the blanks with keywords.

HINT: The answer words rhyme with the italicized words.

1. I've just *written* the cutest story about a _____.

2. My dog, *Barry*, likes to _____ his bone everywhere he goes.

3. Turn left by the *hollow* tree, then _____ the path.

4. When Sonya's in a _____, she moves so fast, she's almost *blurry*.

5. Don't _____ about Fido getting cold. He's really *furry*!

6. I've never *gotten* even a card from Aunt Jill. Isn't that _____?

7. My dad starts to _____ when he gets hot under the *collar*.

Mix & Match

In each box, MATCH a syllable on the left with a syllable on the right to make a word. DRAW a line between the two syllables to match them. REWRITE the words you matched in the blanks.

HINT: All the words have a double consonant in the middle.

at	rent		1. _____
ban	lion		2. _____
col	tack		3. _____
cur	lect		4. _____
mil	ner		5. _____

pos	low		6. _____
pol	ter		7. _____
tun	lute		8. _____
yel	nel		9. _____
scat	sess		10. _____

Spotlight on Consonants and Vowels

You know the difference between a consonant and a vowel, right? Let's check your skills.

List all the consonants in the alphabet:

_____

_____

_____

List all the vowels in the alphabet:

_____

Stack Up

SORT the words into the categories. PUT the words in each list in alphabetical order.

| creepy | hobby | lasso | scooper | merry |
| sputter | needle | aardvark | skiing | upper |

Double Consonants
Example: puppy

1. _____

2. _____

3. _____

4. _____

5. _____

Double Vowels
Example: steeple

1. _____

2. _____

3. _____

4. _____

5. _____

 **Check It!**

Cut out the Check It! section on page 5, and see if you got the answers right.

Keywords

When you spell a word, first break it into SYLLABLES. Usually each syllable has one vowel sound. That vowel sound is a good clue to how to spell the syllable.

READ the paragraph. The words in **bold** are your keywords.

Last **winter**, I went to see the circus. First, there was a **lady** acrobat wearing a pretty **costume** made of sparkly **fabric**. Then, the clowns ran out dressed like cowboys at a **rodeo**. One of them was riding a giant **chicken**! In the **final** act of the **program**, a magician covered an empty **basket** with a soft **velvet** scarf and then waved his wand. When he pulled the scarf away, there was a baby **tiger** inside! What a **super** show!

FILL IN the blanks with the **bold** words in alphabetical order.

1. _____

2. _____

3. _____

4. _____

5. _____

6. _____

7. _____

8. _____

9. _____

10. _____

11. _____

12. _____

Stack Up

You know that in the word *baker*, the vowel sound of the first syllable is a LONG **a**. A long **a** says its name. In the word *banker*, the first vowel sound is a SHORT **a**.

READ the keywords out loud. SORT them by the vowel sound in their first syllable.

basket	chicken	costume	fabric	final	lady
program	rodeo	super	tiger	velvet	winter

Long Vowel Sound	**Short Vowel Sound**
Example: paper	*Example: pamper*
1. _____	1. _____
2. _____	2. _____
3. _____	3. _____
4. _____	4. _____
5. _____	5. _____
6. _____	6. _____

Split It!

SPLIT the keywords into syllables, using dots to mark the breaks.

HINT: If the vowel is long, the syllable usually ends in a vowel. If the vowel is short, the syllable usually ends in a consonant.

Examples: fi•nal, fin•ish

basket	1. _____
chicken	2. _____
costume	3. _____
fabric	4. _____
final	5. _____
lady	6. _____

program	7. _____
rodeo	8. _____
super	9. _____
tiger	10. _____
velvet	11. _____
winter	12. _____

Add It Up

ADD the letters to the middle of the words to make new words. Then SPLIT the new words into syllables, using dots to mark the breaks.

Example: baker: ba•ker + n = ban•ker

1. miser + t = _____   _____

2. gable + m = _____   _____

3. super + p = _____   _____

4. duty   + s = _____   _____

5. fiber + b = _____   _____

6. polar + p = _____   _____

7. unit   + f = _____   _____

Blank Out!

FILL IN the blanks with the words.

evil	exit	hotel	honor	label
level	standards	student	vapors	vanish

1. Shanice does her homework, so she's a good _____.

2. The _____ on my shirt says "dry clean only."

3. We sang a song in _____ of soldiers who died in wars.

4. The hamster must be somewhere. He didn't just _____!

5. If there's a fire, use the emergency _____.

6. Instead of camping, we stayed in a _____.

7. Coach Patel is always talking about our team's high _____.

8. Tonya may be bad, but she's not _____.

9. The factory gives off steam and other _____.

10. Tory is already on _____ 3 of the videogame.

Pick the One!

CIRCLE the word in each pair that starts with a syllable that has a long vowel. SPLIT both words into syllables by drawing a line to mark the break.

Example: (hu|man)   *hum|ble*

1. e x i t   e v i l

2. h o t e l   h o n o r

3. l a b e l   l e v e l

4. s t a n d a r d s   s t u d e n t

5. v a p o r   v a n i s h

✔ Check It!

Cut out the Check It! section on page 9, and see if you got the answers right.

Keywords

The word *oodles* means "a lot." There are oodles of words that end in a consonant + "-le" (like *noodle*, *bottle*, or *pickle*). We'll call them OODLES. In most oodles, the syllable split comes right before the consonant + "-le" (like jun•gle).

READ the paragraph. The words in **bold** are your keywords.

I read a good book with a **purple** cover. The **title** was *Life in 1865*. Imagine living in the **middle** of the 1800s. Instead of driving a car, you'd go to the **stable**, and put a **saddle** and a **bridle** on a horse and ride it. You might have a whole herd of **cattle** or just one cow for milk. You'd make your own clothes using a **needle** and thread, with a **thimble** to protect your finger. At night you'd have to put a **candle** on the dinner **table** for light. Could you **handle** all that?

FILL IN the blanks with the **bold** words in alphabetical order.

1. _____

2. _____

3. _____

4. _____

5. _____

6. _____

7. _____

8. _____

9. _____

10. _____

11. _____

12. _____

✓ Check It!

Page 13

Keywords

1. bridle
2. candle
3. cattle
4. handle
5. middle
6. needle
7. purple
8. saddle
9. stable
10. table
11. thimble
12. title

Page 14

Split It!

1. bri•dle
2. can•dle
3. cat•tle
4. han•dle
5. mid•dle
6. nee•dle
7. pur•ple
8. sad•dle
9. sta•ble
10. ta•ble
11. thim•ble
12. ti•tle

Page 15

Spell Check

1. saddle
2. bridle
3. cattle
4. stable

Mix & Match

1. circle
2. juggle
3. tremble
4. castle
5. twinkle
6. waffle
7. chuckle
8. cradle

Page 16

Stack Up

Long Vowel	Oodles
1. a•pron	1. rum•ble
2. mu•sic	2. sprin•kle
3. pro•duce	3. tem•ple
4. pri•vate	4. gen•tle

Double Consonants

1. pat•tern
2. con•nect
3. les•son
4. ban•ner

Split It!

Oodles follow all the rules you've already learned. SPLIT the keywords into syllables, using dots to mark the breaks.

Example: lit•tle ca•ble twin•kle

bridle	1. _____
candle	2. _____
cattle	3. _____
handle	4. _____
middle	5. _____
needle	6. _____
purple	7. _____
saddle	8. _____
stable	9. _____
table	10. _____
thimble	11. _____
title	12. _____

Spell Check

READ the ad. CIRCLE the four keywords that are misspelled. FILL IN the blanks with those misspelled words. Spell them right!

Big Sale at Bubba's Horse Center!

Need a new sadel? We've got the best! How about a bridel? We've got that too!

We've even got cowboy gear for all you cattel ranchers! All our staybel items are

half-priced! We're not horsing around at Bubba's!

1. _____ 3. _____

2. _____ 4. _____

Mix & Match

MATCH a syllable on the left with a syllable on the right to make a word. DRAW a line between the two syllables to match them. REWRITE the words you matched in the blanks.

Example: an gle → angle

cir	le
jug	fle
trem	dle
cas	kle
twin	tle
waf	gle
chuck	cle
cra	ble

1. _____

2. _____

3. _____

4. _____

5. _____

6. _____

7. _____

8. _____

Stack Up

SORT the words into the categories. SPLIT the words into syllables, using dots to mark the breaks.

rumble	connect	apron	music	private	pattern
sprinkle	produce	lesson	temple	banner	gentle

Long Vowel in First Syllable
Example: bak•er

1. _____

2. _____

3. _____

4. _____

Oodles
Example: cir•cle

1. _____

2. _____

3. _____

4. _____

Double Consonants
Example: mid•dle

1. _____

2. _____

3. _____

4. _____

 **Check It!**

Cut out Check It! to see if you got the answers right.

Pick the One!

CIRCLE the correct syllable split in each pair.

Example: (jun•gle) jung•le

1. me•tal   met•al
2. dra•gon   drag•on
3. fin•ish   fi•nish
4. se•cond   sec•ond
5. ho•nest   hon•est
6. hu•man   hum•an
7. le•vel   lev•el
8. stu•dent   stud•ent

Add It Up

ADD UP the smaller words to make compound words. SPLIT the new words into syllables. FILL IN the blanks, using dots to mark the breaks.

Example: rattle + snake = rat•tle•snake

gentle + man =	1. _____
butter + milk =	2. _____
news + paper =	3. _____
pepper + mint =	4. _____
human + kind =	5. _____
sky + rocket =	6. _____
jelly + fish =	7. _____
motor + cycle =	8. _____

Grid Lock

Here's a list of compound words:

basketball   supermarket   butterfly   grandmother

grasshopper   afternoon   watermelon   fingertip

underground   ladybug

FILL IN the grid with the compound words, writing one letter in each box starting from the left. Be sure to put each word in a row of the right length.

HINT: Pay close attention to where the syllable dots are in the row.

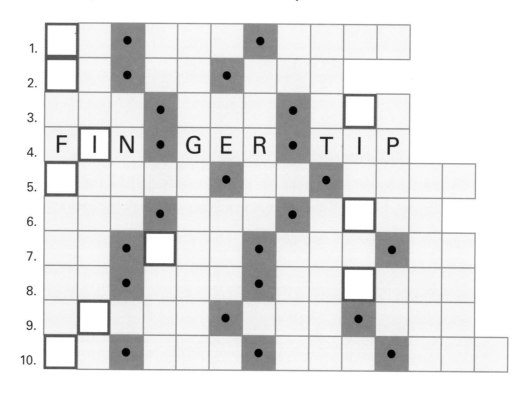

Bonus

The highlighted boxes spell the word for a bunch of large reptiles with snapping jaws. What's the word?

✓ Check It!

Cut out Check It! to see if you got the answers right.

Keywords

Any special ending that you add to a word to change its meaning (even a little) is called a SUFFIX.

A VERB is an action word, like *run* or *sit* or *yell*. Verbs have different suffixes depending on who is doing the action and when:

Verb	*yell*
Add "-s"	He yells.
Add "-ing"	I am yelling now.
Add "-ed"	I yelled yesterday.

READ the paragraph. The words in **bold** are your keywords.

I love a barbecue! Mom **greets** the guests and **boils** the corn while Dad **grills** the burgers. I always have to **remind** him to **melt** some cheese on mine! Our dog loves to **smell** the meat while it **cooks**. After dinner, the grownups **talk** and the little kids **scatter** all over the backyard to **play** games. Soon everyone is **screaming** for dessert. I **want** to eat barbecue every day!

FILL IN the blanks with the **bold** words in alphabetical order.

1. _____   7. _____

2. _____   8. _____

3. _____   9. _____

4. _____   10. _____

5. _____   11. _____

6. _____   12. _____

Bonus

CIRCLE the other verbs in the paragraph.

✓ Check It!

Page 19

Keywords

1. boils	7. remind
2. cooks	8. scatter
3. greets	9. screaming
4. grills	10. smell
5. melt	11. talk
6. play	12. want

Bonus: love, have, loves, is, eat

Page 20

Alternate Endings

+ "-s"	+ "-ing"	+ "-ed"
1. boils	boiling	boiled
2. cooks	cooking	cooked
3. greets	greeting	greeted
4. grills	grilling	grilled
5. melts	melting	melted
6. plays	playing	played
7. reminds	reminding	reminded
8. scatters	scattering	scattered
9. screams	screaming	screamed
10. smells	smelling	smelled
11. talks	talking	talked
12. wants	wanting	wanted

Page 21

Write It Right!

1. greeted	4. melted
2. boiled	5. reminded
3. scattered	6. smelled

Alternate Endings Again!

+ "-s"	+ "-ing"	+ "-ed"
1. attends	attending	attended
2. barks	barking	barked
3. collects	collecting	collected
4. knocks	knocking	knocked
5. groans	groaning	groaned
6. warns	warning	warned

Verbs, Verbing, Verbed

✓ Check It!

Page 22

Pick the One!

1. began	6. got
2. heard	7. said
3. saw	8. took
4. thought	9. knew
5. bought	10. did

Blank Out!

1. knew	4. bought
2. began	5. heard
3. thought	

Alternate Endings

ADD the three endings to the keyword verbs.

Example: act   acts   acting   acted

Verb		Verb + "-s"	Verb + "-ing"	Verb + "-ed"
boil	1.	_____	_____	_____
cook	2.	_____	_____	_____
greet	3.	_____	_____	_____
grill	4.	_____	_____	_____
melt	5.	_____	_____	_____
play	6.	_____	_____	_____
remind	7.	_____	_____	_____
scatter	8.	_____	_____	_____
scream	9.	_____	_____	_____
smell	10.	_____	_____	_____
talk	11.	_____	_____	_____
want	12.	_____	_____	_____

Write It Right!

READ each sentence. UNSCRAMBLE the **bold** word. FILL IN the blanks with the unscrambled words. HINT: All of the words use the past tense "-ed" verb ending.

1. My teammates **tergede** me with a cheer as soon as I walked in.

   _ _ _ _ _ _ _ _

2. Do you like hot dogs grilled or **delobi**?

   _ _ _ _ _ _

3. The papers I dropped **testardec** in the wind.

   _ _ _ _ _ _ _ _ _

4. The snowman **temdle** in the sun.

   _ _ _ _ _ _

5. I'm glad you **merddine** me about the party tonight.

   _ _ _ _ _ _ _ _

6. Clinton **lemsled** so bad after the game, we told him to hit the shower!

   _ _ _ _ _ _ _

Alternate Endings Again!

ADD "-s," "-ing," and "-ed" to these verbs. FILL IN the blanks with the new words.

Example: start   starts   starting   started

Verb	Verb + "-s"	Verb + "-ing"	Verb + "-ed"
attend	1. _____	_____	_____
bark	2. _____	_____	_____
collect	3. _____	_____	_____
knock	4. _____	_____	_____
groan	5. _____	_____	_____
warn	6. _____	_____	_____

Verbs, Verbing, Verbed

Pick the One!

Instead of adding "-ed" to the end of a verb to make it happen in the past, sometimes you have to change the spelling of the whole verb. One example is *run*. The past tense of *run* is *ran*.

CIRCLE the correct past tense verb form of the word in the box.

Example: run   runned   (ran)   ranned

1. begin	began	beginned	beganned
2. hear	heard	heared	herded
3. see	seed	sawed	saw
4. think	thought	thinked	thoughted
5. buy	buyed	bought	boughten
6. get	gat	getted	got
7. say	said	sayed	sed
8. take	taked	toked	took
9. know	knew	knowed	knewed
10. do	doed	done	did

Blank Out!

FILL IN the blanks with oddball verbs.

1. I was sure that I _____ this guy, but I couldn't remember his name.

2. When the starter waved his flag, the race _____.

3. I _____ about the party all day before deciding not to go.

4. Stefan went to the store and _____ a new hat.

5. I'm not sure what I _____, but it sounded loud and scary.

Keywords

To make words PLURAL (more than one), you usually just add an "-s." But when a word ends in "ch," "sh," "x," "o," or "ss," you usually add "-es" to make it plural. Adding "-es" often adds a syllable.

READ the paragraph. The words in **bold** are your keywords.

Dad and I take long **hikes** in the country. We set out early, carrying our **lunches**. We pass through **fields** and small towns with white **churches**. Sometimes we pick **bunches** of **flowers** to bring home to Mom. One time, we saw a pair of **foxes** standing **inches** away from us. I ask Dad a lot of **questions** about the things we see, and he always has good **answers**. He says we should all be **students** of nature. When we get back to the car, we treat ourselves like **heroes** and get a big pizza dinner. That's the best part of the day!

FILL IN the blanks with the **bold** words in alphabetical order.

1. _____   7. _____

2. _____   8. _____

3. _____   9. _____

4. _____   10. _____

5. _____   11. _____

6. _____   12. _____

✓ Check It!

Page 23

Keywords

1. answers
2. bunches
3. churches
4. fields
5. flowers
6. foxes
7. heroes
8. hikes
9. inches
10. lunches
11. questions
12. students

Page 24

Stack Up

"-s" Plurals
1. an•swers
2. fields
3. flow•ers
4. hikes
5. ques•tions
6. stu•dents

"-es" Plurals
1. bunch•es
2. church•es
3. fox•es
4. he•roes
5. inch•es
6. lunch•es

Page 25

Spell Check

1. bunches
2. inches
3. heroes
4. lunches
5. questions
6. flowers

Alternate Endings

1. beaches
2. blankets
3. chapters
4. flashes
5. fountains
6. guests
7. lobsters
8. masses
9. porches
10. potatoes
11. servants
12. successes

Page 26

Spotlight on More Verb Endings

1. matches
2. mixes
3. brushes
4. wishes
5. stitches
6. presses
7. confesses
8. reaches
9. attaches
10. relaxes
11. rushes
12. vanishes

Stack Up

READ the keywords out loud. SORT the keywords by their plural endings. SPLIT the words into syllables (if they have more than one), using dots to mark the breaks.

HINT: The syllable break *usually* comes before the "-es" plural ending.

Example: socks   dress•es

answers	bunches	churches	fields	flowers	foxes
heroes	hikes	inches	lunches	questions	students

"-s" Plurals	**"-es" Plurals**
1. _____	1. _____
2. _____	2. _____
3. _____	3. _____
4. _____	4. _____
5. _____	5. _____
6. _____	6. _____

6

Spell Check

READ the diary entry. CIRCLE the six keywords that are misspelled.
FILL IN the blanks with those misspelled words. Spell them right!

Dear Diary:

I messed up everything today! I made bunchiz of mistakes on my history test.
And I couldn't make centimeters into inchiz in math class. In English, we had to
talk about our heerose, and I didn't have any. When Stefanie and I were eating
our lunchiz, she kept asking me kwestionz about stuff I didn't know. Worst of all, I
forgot to get floworz for Mom's birthday. Am I a total doofus, or what?

1. _____   4. _____

2. _____   5. _____

3. _____   6. _____

Alternate Endings

ADD the "-s" or "-es" ending to these words to make them plural.

HINT: Remember, if the word ends in "ch," "sh," "x," "o," or "ss," it takes "-es."

Example: bug   bugs

Singular	Plural	Singular	Plural
beach	1. _____	lobster	7. _____
blanket	2. _____	mass	8. _____
chapter	3. _____	porch	9. _____
flash	4. _____	potato	10. _____
fountain	5. _____	servant	11. _____
guest	6. _____	success	12. _____

Spotlight on More Verb Endings

The "-es" rule goes for verbs too. So when a verb ends in "ch," "sh," "x," "o," or "ss," you usually need to add "-es" to make it the right form. This usually adds a syllable. Try it out!

ADD "-es" to each verb.

Example: fix   fixes

Verb	Verb + "-es"
match	1. _____
mix	2. _____
brush	3. _____
wish	4. _____
stitch	5. _____
press	6. _____
confess	7. _____
reach	8. _____
attach	9. _____
relax	10. _____
rush	11. _____
vanish	12. _____

Keywords

When a word ends in "y," you have to drop the "y" and add "-ies" to make it a plural. This does not usually add a syllable. For example, *(lady – y) + ies = ladies.*

READ the paragraph. The words in **bold** are your keywords.

My uncle owns two **companies** that make snowboards. He has **factories** in five different **countries** and offices in many big **cities**. More and more **families** are snowboarding nowadays. I've even seen a few **babies** learning how! People like nothing better than stretching their **bodies** to the limit, flying down a mountain under clear, blue **skies**. But many skiers who own **properties** in mountain **communities** complain that snowboarders are taking over their **territories** and refusing to share the slopes. They tell **stories** of accidents caused by rude behavior. Everyone needs to be careful.

FILL IN the blanks with the **bold** words in alphabetical order.

1. _____
2. _____
3. _____
4. _____
5. _____
6. _____
7. _____
8. _____
9. _____
10. _____
11. _____
12. _____

 **Check It!**

Page 30

**Spotlight on Verbs
That End in "Y"**

+ "-s"	+ "-ing"	+ "-ed"
1. buries	burying	buried
2. carries	carrying	carried
3. dries	drying	dried
4. fries	frying	fried
5. empties	emptying	emptied
6. hurries	hurrying	hurried
7. marries	marrying	married
8. tries	trying	tried
9. worries	worrying	worried

Alternate Endings

FILL IN the blanks with the singular forms of the keywords.

Example: ladies   lady

Plural	**Singular**
babies	1. _____
bodies	2. _____
cities	3. _____
communities	4. _____
companies	5. _____
countries	6. _____
factories	7. _____
families	8. _____
properties	9. _____
skies	10. _____
stories	11. _____
territories	12. _____

Write It Right!

UNSCRAMBLE the keywords. HINT: They all end in "-ies."

1. My family has visitied all the jellybean **seftocari** in California.

   _ _ □ _ _ _ _ _ _

2. My grandpa tells lots of great **irestos** about my parents.

   _ _ □ _ _ _ _

3. The people around here don't like when I walk my dog on their **tippeesorr**.

   □ _ _ _ _ _ _ _ _ _

4. Many **usimminocet** have a neighborhood watch program.

   _ _ _ _ _ _ _ □ _ _ _

5. Someday, I want to travel to lots of foreign **stirounce**.

   _ _ _ _ _ _ □ _ _

6. My parents both work for computer **pomnicesa**.

   _ _ _ _ _ _ _ □ _

Bonus: The boxed letters spell twins, triplets, or clones!

□ □ □ □ □ □

Alternate Endings

DROP the "y" and ADD an "-ies" to each word to make it plural. WRITE the new words.

Singular	Plural	Singular	Plural
blueberry	1. _____	diary	7. _____
bunny	2. _____	library	8. _____
butterfly	3. _____	memory	9. _____
century	4. _____	mystery	10. _____
colony	5. _____	penny	11. _____
copy	6. _____	society	12. _____

Spotlight on Verbs That End in "Y"

Just like nouns that end in "y," when a verb ends in "y" (like *cry*), you have to drop the "y" and add "-ies" or "-ied" to get the right form. Be careful: You leave the "y" when you add "-ing."

FILL IN the blanks with the correct verb forms.

Example: cry   cries   crying   cried

Verb	Verb + "-s"	Verb + "-ing"	Verb + "-ed"
bury	1. _____	_____	_____
carry	2. _____	_____	_____
dry	3. _____	_____	_____
fry	4. _____	_____	_____
empty	5. _____	_____	_____
hurry	6. _____	_____	_____
marry	7. _____	_____	_____
try	8. _____	_____	_____
worry	9. _____	_____	_____

Keywords

Here are two more rules about plural suffixes:

Rule 1: If a word ends in an "f," then you have to drop the "f" and add "-ves" to make it plural. This usually does not add a syllable.

So: *(calf – f) + ves = calves*

Or: *(knife – fe) + ves = knives*

Rule 2: Some words have weird plurals, like *foot* and *feet*.

READ the paragraph. The words in **bold** are your keywords.

In the old days, farm families lived very busy **lives**. They took care of their animals, including the **calves**, **geese**, and **oxen**. They groomed their horses and checked their **teeth** and **hooves**. Dogs guarded against **wolves**. Cats kept **mice** out of the grain. While the **men** tended the fields, their **wives** made everything from **loaves** of bread to butter. Even the **children** had jobs to do!

FILL IN the blanks with the **bold** words in alphabetical order.

1. _____

2. _____

3. _____

4. _____

5. _____

6. _____

7. _____

8. _____

9. _____

10. _____

11. _____

12. _____

✓ Check It!

Page 31

Keywords

1. calves
2. children
3. geese
4. hooves
5. lives
6. loaves
7. men
8. mice
9. oxen
10. teeth
11. wives
12. wolves

Page 32

Stack Up

"-f" to "-ves" Plurals

Plural	Singular
1. calves	calf
2. hooves	hoof
3. lives	life
4. loaves	loaf
5. wives	wife
6. wolves	wolf

Oddball Plurals

Plural	Singular
1. children	child
2. geese	goose
3. men	man
4. mice	mouse
5. oxen	ox
6. teeth	tooth

Page 33

Criss Cross

ACROSS	DOWN
2. men	1. oxen
4. children	2. mice
5. teeth	3. geese

Alternate Endings

1. dwarves	5. scarves
2. halves	6. selves
3. knives	7. shelves
4. leaves	8. thieves

Even More Plurals

✓ **Check It!**

Page 34

Spotlight on Syllables

One-Syllable Words	Two-Syllable Words
1. scarves	1. ditch•es
2. knives	2. bush•es
3. dice	3. ox•en
4. moves	4. branch•es
5. flies	5. box•es
6. hooves	6. inch•es

Stack Up

READ the keywords out loud. SORT the keywords by how they become plural. Then FILL IN the blanks with the singular forms of the words.

| calves | children | geese | hooves | lives | loaves |
| men | mice | oxen | teeth | wives | wolves |

"-f" to "-ves" Plurals
Example: knives   knife

Plural	Singular
1. _____	_____
2. _____	_____
3. _____	_____
4. _____	_____
5. _____	_____
6. _____	_____

Oddball Plurals
Example: feet foot

Plural	Singular
1. _____	_____
2. _____	_____
3. _____	_____
4. _____	_____
5. _____	_____
6. _____	_____

Criss Cross

FILL IN the grid by answering the clues with keywords.

ACROSS

2. More than one man

4. More than one child

5. More than one tooth

DOWN

1. More than one ox

2. More than one mouse

3. More than one goose

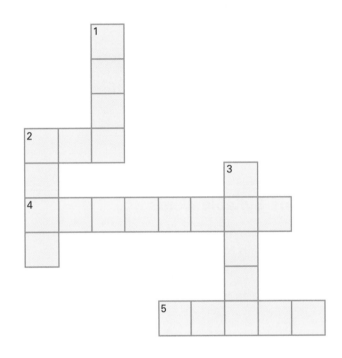

Alternate Endings

DROP the "f" or "fe" and ADD a "-ves" to these words to make them plural.
FILL IN the blanks with the plural words.

Example: life   lives

Singular		Plural	Singular		Plural
dwarf	1.	_____	scarf	5.	_____
half	2.	_____	self	6.	_____
knife	3.	_____	shelf	7.	_____
leaf	4.	_____	thief	8.	_____

Spotlight on Syllables

READ these plural words out loud. SORT the words by how many syllables they have. SPLIT the words into syllables, using dots to mark the breaks.

ditches	bushes	scarves	oxen	branches	knives
dice	moves	flies	hooves	boxes	inches

Example: slots   spac•es

One-Syllable Words	**Two-Syllable Words**
1. _____	1. _____
2. _____	2. _____
3. _____	3. _____
4. _____	4. _____
5. _____	5. _____
6. _____	6. _____

Word Search

FILL IN the blanks with the plural versions of the words listed. Then CIRCLE these plural words in the word grid. Words go down and across, not diagonally or backwards.

Example: lady   ladies

Singular	Plural
pillow	1. _____
cherry	2. _____
switch	3. _____
torch	4. _____
goose	5. _____
thief	6. _____
shelf	7. _____
mouse	8. _____
lasso	9. _____
penny	10. _____

```
R  V  S  W  I  T  C  H  E  S  L
O  T  H  I  E  V  E  S  G  Z  A
S  X  E  T  O  R  C  H  E  S  S
P  I  L  L  O  W  S  P  E  M  S
Q  W  V (L  A  D  I  E  S) I  O
C  H  E  R  R  I  E  S  E  C  E
M  Y  S  U  P  E  N  N  I  E  S
```

Split It!

SPLIT the compound words into syllables, using dots to mark the breaks.

newspapers	1. _____
grandchildren	2. _____
superheroes	3. _____
princesses	4. _____
lunchboxes	5. _____
battleships	6. _____
earthquakes	7. _____
housewives	8. _____

Alternate Endings

ADD the suffixes to the verbs listed.

Example: yell yells yelling yelled

Verb		Verb + "-s"	Verb + "-ing"	Verb + "-ed"
empty	1.	_____	_____	_____
search	2.	_____	_____	_____
approach	3.	_____	_____	_____
bury	4.	_____	_____	_____
display	5.	_____	_____	_____
establish	6.	_____	_____	_____

Keywords

Adjectives are words that describe things, like *cool*. To say that ferrets are *cooler* than dogs, we make *cool* into a COMPARATIVE by adding the suffix "-er." To say llamas are the *coolest* pets of all, we make *cool* into a SUPERLATIVE by adding the suffix "-est."

READ the paragraph. The words in **bold** are your keywords.

In my family, Trisha is the **oldest**. She thinks she's **smarter** than everyone. My sister Ann is the **quietest** and **neatest** person ever! Derek is the **youngest**, but he's **taller** than I am. Mom says I'm the **wildest** one, and she wishes I were **calmer** and **cleaner**, like Ann. In sports, Dad can throw **longer**, but Derek is **quicker**, and I'm **stronger**. We have a lot of fun together.

FILL IN the blanks with the **bold** words in alphabetical order.

1. _____

2. _____

3. _____

4. _____

5. _____

6. _____

7. _____

8. _____

9. _____

10. _____

11. _____

12. _____

Check It!

Page 37

Keywords

1. calmer
2. cleaner
3. longer
4. neatest
5. oldest
6. quicker
7. quietest
8. smarter
9. stronger
10. taller
11. wildest
12. youngest

Page 38

Alternate Endings

	Comparative	Superlative
1.	calmer	calmest
2.	cleaner	cleanest
3.	longer	longest
4.	neater	neatest
5.	older	oldest
6.	quicker	quickest
7.	quieter	quietest
8.	smarter	smartest
9.	stronger	strongest
10.	taller	tallest
11.	wilder	wildest
12.	younger	youngest

Page 39

Word Blocks

1. calmer		4. neatest	
2. wilder		5. younger	
3. quickest		6. cleanest	

Alternate Endings Again!

	Comparative	Superlative
1.	brighter	brightest
2.	cheaper	cheapest
3.	higher	highest
4.	smoother	smoothest
5.	weaker	weakest
6.	blinder	blindest

Cool, Cooler, Coolest

✓ Check It!

Page 40

Spotlight on Something Fishy

1. tricky
2. brainy
3. gloomy
4. moody
5. satiny
6. silky
7. stumpy
8. smelly
9. wealthy
10. worthy
11. sweaty
12. shadowy

Bonus:

1. wrinkly
2. wiry
3. spongy
4. nobly
5. slimy

Alternate Endings

ADD the comparative and superlative suffix to each of the words.

Example: cool   cooler   coolest

Word	Comparative	Superlative
calm	1. _____	_____
clean	2. _____	_____
long	3. _____	_____
neat	4. _____	_____
old	5. _____	_____
quick	6. _____	_____
quiet	7. _____	_____
smart	8. _____	_____
strong	9. _____	_____
tall	10. _____	_____
wild	11. _____	_____
young	12. _____	_____

Word Blocks

One way to remember the spelling of a word is to picture its shape. Word blocks are a good way to practice.

Example: | p | e | n | c | i | l |

FILL IN the word blocks with words of the same shape from the list.

HINT: Look for double consonants and watch out for the word endings.

| calmer | neatest | cleanest | younger | quickest | wilder |

1. ☐
2. ☐
3. ☐
4. ☐
5. ☐
6. ☐

Alternate Endings Again!

ADD the suffixes to make the words into comparatives and superlatives.

Example: round   rounder   roundest

Word	Comparative	Superlative
bright	1. _____	_____
cheap	2. _____	_____
high	3. _____	_____
smooth	4. _____	_____
weak	5. _____	_____
blind	6. _____	_____

Spotlight on Something "Fish-y"

Suffixes can make a singular into a plural or an adjective into a superlative. You can also use suffixes to transform an ordinary noun, like *fish*, into an adjective just by adding "-y" to the end: *fishy*.

ADD "-y" to these nouns to make them into adjectives.

Example: fish   fishy

Noun	Adjective		Noun	Adjective
trick	1. _____		stump	7. _____
brain	2. _____		smell	8. _____
gloom	3. _____		wealth	9. _____
mood	4. _____		worth	10. _____
satin	5. _____		sweat	11. _____
silk	6. _____		shadow	12. _____

Bonus

When a word ends in "e," you usually drop the "e" before adding the "-y."

Example: scale   scaly

Noun	Adjective
wrinkle	1. _____
wire	2. _____
sponge	3. _____
noble	4. _____
slime	5. _____

Keywords

When a verb ends in a single vowel followed by a single consonant (like *tag*), you usually have to double the consonant before you add the verb endings "-ed" and "-ing." For example, *tag, tagged, tagging*.

READ the paragraph. The words in **bold** are your keywords.

Tonight I **starred** in the school play! I played a girl who was **planning** to leave home until her mother **begged** her to stay. At first I was **gripped** with fear and kept **skipping** lines. Then I **ripped** my costume, but we **pinned** it up backstage. Between acts I **grabbed** some food and water. I was afraid the show had **flopped**, but everyone **clapped** like crazy. Afterward people kept **stopping** by and **hugging** me. It was a success!

FILL IN the blanks with the **bold** words in alphabetical order.

1. _____
2. _____
3. _____
4. _____
5. _____
6. _____

7. _____
8. _____
9. _____
10. _____
11. _____
12. _____

✓ **Check It!**

Page 41
Keywords

1. begged
2. clapped
3. flopped
4. grabbed
5. gripped
6. hugging
7. pinned
8. planning
9. ripped
10. skipping
11. starred
12. stopping

Page 42
Alternate Endings

+ "s"	+ "-ing"	+ "-ed"
1. begs	begging	begged
2. claps	clapping	clapped
3. flops	flopping	flopped
4. grabs	grabbing	grabbed
5. grips	gripping	gripped
6. hugs	hugging	hugged
7. pins	pinning	pinned
8. plans	planning	planned
9. rips	ripping	ripped
10. skips	skipping	skipped
11. stars	starring	starred
12. stops	stopping	stopped

Page 43
Spell Check

1. skipped   3. grabbed
2. clapped   4. hugged

Stack Up

One-Syllable Words	Two-Syllable Words
1. begged	1. clap•ping
2. flopped	2. grab•bing
3. gripped	3. hug•ging
4. pinned	4. plan•ning
5. ripped	5. skip•ping
6. stopped	6. star•ring

Alternate Endings

ADD the suffixes to make each verb form.

HINT: You'll have to double the final consonant of each verb.

Example: tag   tags   tagging   tagged

Check It!

Page 44

Spotlight on Comparatives and Superlatives

Comparative	Superlative
1. wetter	wettest
2. fatter	fattest
3. fitter	fittest
4. hotter	hottest
5. madder	maddest
6. redder	reddest
7. sadder	saddest
8. slimmer	slimmest
9. tanner	tannest
10. thinner	thinnest

Verb		Verb + "s"	Verb + "-ing"	Verb + "-ed"
beg	1.	begs	begging	bedded
clap	2.	claps	clapping	clapped
flop	3.	flops	flopping	flopped
grab	4.	grabs	grabbing	grabbed
grip	5.	grips	gripping	gribbed
hug	6.	hugs	hugging	hugged
pin	7.	pins	pinning	pinned
plan	8.	plans	planning	planned
rip	9.	rips	ripping	ripped
skip	10.	skips	skipping	skipped
star	11.	stars	staring	stared
stop	12.	stops	stopping	stopped

Spell Check

READ the diary entry. CIRCLE the four words that are misspelled. Then FILL IN the blanks with those misspelled words. Spell them right!

> Dear Diary:
>
> Today, Shanice and I (skiped) to the bus stop and sang a song to all the kids. Everyone (claped) along. Then, Shanice (grabed) Michael's hat, and we tossed it around. When we got on the bus, Shanice (huged) me and told me I was her best friend!

1. clapped
2. skipped
3. hugged
4. grabbed

Stack Up

READ the words out loud. SORT them by how many syllables they have. FILL IN the blanks with the sorted words. SPLIT the words into syllables, using dots to mark the breaks.

HINT: Remember the double consonants!

| begged | clapping | flopped | grabbing | gripped | hugging |
| pinned | planning | ripped | skipping | starring | stopped |

One-Syllable Words
Example: clipped

1. begged
2. pinned
3. flopped
4. ripped
5. gripped
6. stopped

Two-Syllable Words
Example: clip•ping

1. clap•ping
2. plan•ning   planning
3. star•ring
4. hug•ging
5. grab•bing
6. skip•ping

Double Consonants Again!

Spotlight on Comparatives and Superlatives

When a word ends in a single vowel and a single consonant, you have to double the consonant before you add "-er" or "-est" to make it a comparative or superlative. For example, *big, bigger, biggest.*

ADD the endings to make the words into comparatives and superlatives. WRITE the new words in the blanks next to the original word.

Example: big   bigger   biggest

Word		Comparative	Superlative
wet	1.	_____	_____
fat	2.	_____	_____
fit	3.	_____	_____
hot	4.	_____	_____
mad	5.	_____	_____
red	6.	_____	_____
sad	7.	_____	_____
slim	8.	_____	_____
tan	9.	_____	_____
thin	10.	_____	_____

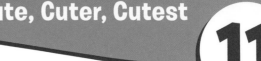
Keywords

When an adjective ends in "e," you have to drop the last "e" before adding "-er" or "-est" to make it a comparative or superlative. For example, (*cute* – e) + er = *cuter*.

READ the paragraph. The words in **bold** are your keywords.

The Amazon Jungle used to be one of the **widest** forests in the world with the **purest** water. It is home to some of the **largest** animals, as well as the **strangest**. One of the **nicer**, **gentler** creatures is the sloth. It lives a **simple** life, eating the **finest** leaves and the **ripest** fruits. The sloth is **happiest** when it's asleep. Sadly, every year the sloth's **safe** world gets **closer** to being destroyed.

FILL IN the blanks with the **bold** words in alphabetical order.

1. _____
2. _____
3. _____
4. _____
5. _____
6. _____

7. _____
8. _____
9. _____
10. _____
11. _____
12. _____

✓ Check It!

Page 45
Keywords

1. closer
2. finest
3. gentler
4. happiest
5. largest
6. nicer
7. purest
8. ripest
9. safe
10. simple
11. strangest
12. widest

Page 46
Alternate Endings

Comparative	Superlative
1. closer	closest
2. finer	finest
3. gentler	gentlest
4. happier	happiest
5. larger	largest
6. nicer	nicest
7. purer	purest
8. riper	ripest
9. safer	safest
10. simpler	simplest
11. stranger	strangest
12. wider	widest

Page 47
Spotlight on Adjectives That End in "Y"

Comparative	Superlative
1. emptier	emptiest
2. fancier	fanciest
3. easier	easiest
4. merrier	merriest
5. trickier	trickiest
6. brainier	brainiest
7. gloomier	gloomiest
8. smellier	smelliest
9. wealthier	wealthiest
10. worthier	worthiest
11. scarier	scariest
12. sweatier	sweatiest

✓ **Check It!**

Page 48

Spotlight on Verbs That End in "E"

+ "-s"	+ "-ing"	+ "-ed"
1. bounces	bouncing	bounced
2. chases	chasing	chased
3. fades	fading	faded
4. hates	hating	hated
5. hopes	hoping	hoped
6. skates	skating	skated
7. smiles	smiling	smiled
8. stares	staring	stared
9. trades	trading	traded
10. trembles	trembling	trembled
11. wages	waging	waged
12. wiggles	wiggling	wiggled

Alternate Endings

ADD the suffixes to the words to make them comparatives and superlatives.

Example: tame   tamer   tamest

Word	Comparative	Superlative
close	1. _____	_____
fine	2. _____	_____
gentle	3. _____	_____
happy	4. _____	_____
large	5. _____	_____
nice	6. _____	_____
pure	7. _____	_____
ripe	8. _____	_____
safe	9. _____	_____
simple	10. _____	_____
strange	11. _____	_____
wide	12. _____	_____

Spotlight on Adjectives That End in "Y"

Remember our magic suffix that made nouns into adjectives? Well, it's *trickier* making adjectives into comparatives and superlatives. To make *happy* into a comparative or superlative, you have to drop the "y" and replace it with an "i." Go for it!

ADD the suffixes to make the words into comparatives and superlatives.

Example: happy   happier   happiest

Word	Comparative	Superlative
empty	1. _____	_____
fancy	2. _____	_____
easy	3. _____	_____
merry	4. _____	_____
tricky	5. _____	_____
brainy	6. _____	_____
gloomy	7. _____	_____
smelly	8. _____	_____
wealthy	9. _____	_____
worthy	10. _____	_____
scary	11. _____	_____
sweaty	12. _____	_____

Spotlight on Verbs That End in "E"

Just like with adjectives, when a verb ends in the letter "e," you have to drop the "e" before adding the "-ed" or "-ing" endings. For example, *like, liking, liked*.

FILL IN the blanks with the correct verb forms.

Example: *wipe   wipes   wiping   wiped*

Verb	Verb + "-s"	Verb + "-ing"	Verb + "-ed"
bounce	1. _____	_____	_____
chase	2. _____	_____	_____
fade	3. _____	_____	_____
hate	4. _____	_____	_____
hope	5. _____	_____	_____
skate	6. _____	_____	_____
smile	7. _____	_____	_____
stare	8. _____	_____	_____
trade	9. _____	_____	_____
tremble	10. _____	_____	_____
wage	11. _____	_____	_____
wiggle	12. _____	_____	_____

Word Blocks

FILL IN the word blocks with words of the same shape from the list.

HINT: Look for double consonants and watch out for the word endings.

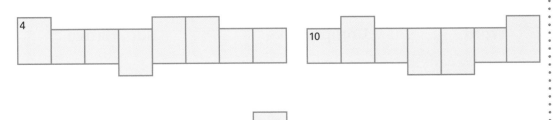

skipped	brighter	giggling	scariest	thinnest
switches	heroes	sprinkle	jungle	halfway

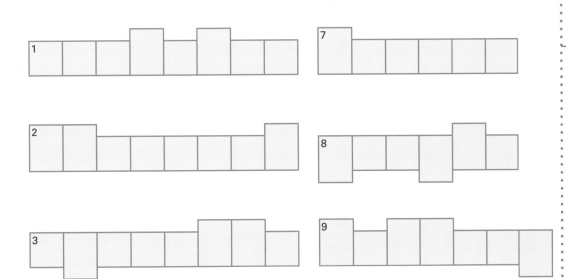

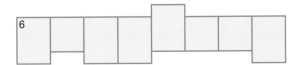

✓ **Check It!**

Page 49

Word Blocks

1. switches
2. thinnest
3. sprinkle
4. brighter
5. scariest
6. giggling
7. hereos
8. jungle
9. halfway
10. skipped

Page 50

Add It Up

1. potatoes   5. carrying
2. skating   6. slapped
3. children   7. leaves
4. ponies   8. flipping

Alternate Endings

Comparative	Superlative
1. barer	barest
2. blonder	blondest
3. braver	bravest
4. gentler	gentlest
5. whiter	whitest

Add It Up

SOLVE the "problems" by adding the correct suffix.

Example: wolf + wolf = wolves

potato + potato =	1. _____
skate + ing =	2. _____
child + child =	3. _____
pony + pony =	4. _____
carry + ing =	5. _____
slap + ed =	6. _____
leaf + leaf =	7. _____
flip + ing =	8. _____

Alternate Endings

ADD the suffixes to the keywords to make them comparatives and superlatives.

Example: cute   cuter   cutest

Word	Comparative	Superlative
bare	1. _____	_____
blonde	2. _____	_____
brave	3. _____	_____
gentle	4. _____	_____
white	5. _____	_____

Keywords

Remember adjectives like *smooth* that describe things? Well, words that describe verbs are called ADVERBS. To make an adverb, just add the suffix "-ly" to the end of an adjective.

READ the paragraph. The words in **bold** are your keywords.

I was **totally** excited about Carla's costume party and **closely** watched the clock at school all day. The minutes ticked by so **slowly**. When I **finally** got home, I changed **rapidly** into my zombie costume. It fit **perfectly**. Everyone on the street looked at me **strangely**. I zipped **quickly** and **happily** to Carla's, where we stayed **mainly** in her backyard. **Sadly**, it started to rain, which **completely** ruined everything. Sigh.

FILL IN the blanks with the **bold** words in alphabetical order.

1. _____
2. _____
3. _____
4. _____
5. _____
6. _____
7. _____
8. _____
9. _____
10. _____
11. _____
12. _____

Split It!

SPLIT the keywords into syllables, using dots to mark the breaks.

HINT: The suffix "-ly" is always its own syllable.

Examples: smooth•ly

closely	1. _____
completely	2. _____
finally	3. _____
happily	4. _____
mainly	5. _____
quickly	6. _____
perfectly	7. _____
rapidly	8. _____
sadly	9. _____
slowly	10. _____
strangely	11. _____
totally	12. _____

Spell Check

READ Alicia's e-mail. CIRCLE the five keywords that are misspelled. FILL IN the blanks with those misspelled words. Spell them right!

TO: Missy

FROM: Alicia

RE: Cheerleader Tryouts—Finaly!

I totaly can't believe you missed tryouts today! Sharon was acting strangeley. She didn't say hi to me when I got there and was manely hanging out with Tye. I kwickilly put a stop to that by asking her what was wrong. She said she thought I didn't want her to make the team. I kompleatly cleared that up and we're friends again!

1. _____   4. _____

2. _____   5. _____

3. _____   6. _____

Alternate Endings

The keywords include the word *happily*. Did you notice that it's not *happyly*? Whenever an adjective ends in a "y," you have to replace the "y" with an "i" before making it an adverb. Try it.

TRANSFORM these adjectives into adverbs.

Example: sporty   sportily

Adjective	Adverb		Adjective	Adverb	
angry	1. _____		pretty	5. _____	
crazy	2. _____		lazy	6. _____	
easy	3. _____		thirsty	7. _____	
hungry	4. _____		speedy	8. _____	

Spotlight on Making People Out of Verbs

Suffixes can turn nouns into adjectives (*sun → sunny*), adjectives into superlatives (*sunny → sunniest*), and adjectives into adverbs (*sunny → sunnily*). But did you know that the suffix "-er" can turn a verb into a noun?

FILL IN the blanks by adding the suffix "-er" to make the **bold** verb into a person.

HINT: Add "-er" to the basic verb form (remove the "-s").

*Example: A person who **works** is a **worker**.*

1. Manny **plays** football, so he's a football _____.

2. If you **shop**, then you're a _____.

3. A person who **teaches** is a _____.

4. Kyle's dad **trains** athletes. He's a _____.

5. If you **perform** on stage, then you're a _____.

6. Someone who **dances** is a _____.

7. Mr. Santos loves to **golf**. He's a _____.

8. If you **groom** dogs, you're a dog _____.

9. A person who **walks** dogs is a dog _____.

10. Roberta **explores** the jungle. She's an _____.

11. Something that **sharpens** pencils is a _____.

12. You use a _____ to **scrape** the ice from your car.

Keywords

Here are three more suffixes for you to enjoy:

"-Ful" means *full of*, so *useful* means *full of use*.

"-Less" means *lacking*, so *useless* means *has no use*.

"-Ness" changes an adjective into a noun. For example: *happy* → *happiness*.

READ the paragraph. The words in **bold** are your keywords.

> My band, Firecracker, was very **grateful** for the chance to play at this year's town fair. It was **wonderful**! We played a **handful** of songs under a **cloudless** sky in the main arena. Our lead singer, Robbie, got over her **shyness** about being on stage and became **fearless**! Then, one of the stage crew was **careless** and pulled out a wire. So we played the rest of the show in **darkness**. The **joyful** crowd loved it and the applause was **plentiful**. The mayor called us "**delightful**." Overall, our first concert was very **successful**!

FILL IN the blanks with the **bold** words in alphabetical order.

1. _____
2. _____
3. _____
4. _____
5. _____
6. _____

7. _____
8. _____
9. _____
10. _____
11. _____
12. _____

Split It!

SPLIT the keywords into syllables, using dots to mark the breaks.

HINT: A suffix is usually its own syllable.

Example: use•ful

careless	1. _____
cloudless	2. _____
darkness	3. _____
delightful	4. _____
fearless	5. _____
grateful	6. _____
handful	7. _____
joyful	8. _____
plentiful	9. _____
shyness	10. _____
successful	11. _____
wonderful	12. _____

Spell Check

READ Carrie's thank-you note. CIRCLE the five keywords that are misspelled.
FILL IN the blanks with those misspelled words. Spell them right!

> Hi Penny.
>
> I had a delitefull time swimming in your wunderfull pool. You are so feerliss in the
>
> deep end! I'm glad the day was clowdiless. By the way, I left my swimsuit in your
>
> bedroom. No wonder Mom calls me "Careliss Carrie!" I'll get it next weekend.
>
> Carrie

1. _____   4. _____

2. _____   5. _____

3. _____

Morph It!

Since "-less" is the opposite of "-ful," then *useless* is the opposite of *useful*. REPLACE "-less" or
"-ful" to make the opposite word. WRITE the opposite word on the blank.

Example: useful   useless

careful	1. _____	graceful	6. _____
pitiful	2. _____	helpless	7. _____
fearful	3. _____	doubtful	8. _____
joyless	4. _____	harmless	9. _____
tasteless	5. _____	faithful	10. _____

Spotlight on Piling on the Suffixes

Suffixes are like potato chips—you can't stop after just one! SPLIT these words into syllables, using dots to mark the breaks.

HINT: Suffixes are usually their own syllable, and each word has more than one suffix.

Example: usefulness   use•ful•ness

skillfully	1. _____
carelessness	2. _____
painlessly	3. _____
hopefulness	4. _____
thankfully	5. _____
thoughtlessly	6. _____
youthfulness	7. _____

Alternate Endings

When you add "-less" or "-ful" to a noun, it becomes an adjective. When you add "-ness" to an adjective, it becomes a noun.

ADD "-less" to the nouns to make them adjectives. ADD "-ness" to the adjectives to make them nouns. WRITE the new words on the blanks.

Example: shy   shyness   Example: cloud   cloudless

thoughtful	1. _____		good	5. _____
polite	2. _____		spot	6. _____
kind	3. _____		sweet	7. _____
home	4. _____		spine	8. _____

Keywords

You sure know your suffixes! Here are some PREFIXES to try out:

"Pre-" means *before*, so *prepay* means *to pay beforehand*.
"Re-" means *again*, so *reheat* means *to heat again*.
"Mis-" means *wrong*, so a *mismatch* is *a wrong match*.
"Un-" means *not*, so *unfair* means *not fair*.

READ the paragraph. The words in **bold** are your keywords.

When you live by a river, flooding is not **uncommon** or **unexpected**. When I was in **preschool**, we were **unlucky**. We took every **precaution**. We had to **rebuild** and **repaint** our house after a big storm. Then, when I was a **preteen**, our basement flooded. I love our river, and it's hard to remember how it can **misbehave** during the rainy season. Its usual calm, flat surface is **misleading**. A lot of new neighbors were **misinformed** about flooding in this area, and they didn't **review** the information available. Boy, were they surprised!

FILL IN the blanks with the **bold** words in alphabetical order.

1. _____   7. _____

2. _____   8. _____

3. _____   9. _____

4. _____   10. _____

5. _____   11. _____

6. _____   12. _____

Criss Cross

FILL IN the grid by answering the clues with keywords.

ACROSS

1. Not expected

2. Build again

3. Behave wrongly

4. Leading the wrong way

DOWN

1. Not common

2. Paint again

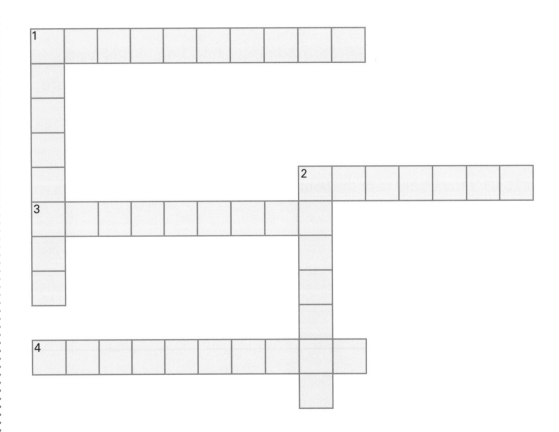

Spell Check

READ the diary entry. CIRCLE the four keywords that are misspelled. FILL IN the blanks with those misspelled words. Spell them right!

> Dear Diary:
>
> My sister failed her driving test again! She took every preekaushun
> too. I even helped her to riview all the rules and signals. But she was
> missinformed about the time of the test, so she was late and nervous.
> Then she ran a red light! She is so unnlucky.

1. _____   3. _____

2. _____   4. _____

Split It!

SPLIT the keywords into syllables, using dots to mark the breaks.

HINT: A prefix is usually one syllable.

Example: predawn, pre•dawn

misbehave	1. _____	rebuild	7. _____
misinformed	2. _____	repaint	8. _____
misleading	3. _____	review	9. _____
preteen	4. _____	uncommon	10. _____
precaution	5. _____	unexpected	11. _____
preschool	6. _____	unlucky	12. _____

Blank Out!

ADD the prefix "pre-," "re-," "mis-," or "un-" to match the definitions. FILL IN the blanks with the new words.

Example: **re**use *means to use again.*

1. _____cook means to cook beforehand

2. _____arrange means to arrange again.

3. _____spell means to spell wrong.

4. _____buttoned means not buttoned.

5. _____game means before the game.

6. _____historic means before recorded hstory.

7. _____invent means to invent again.

8. _____place means to put in the wrong place.

9. _____familiar means not familiar.

10. _____treat means to treat badly.

Bonus

The prefix "sub-" means *under* or *less than.*

ADD the prefix "sub-" to match the definition.

1. A _____way train goes under the ground.

2. _____zero temperatures are less than zero degrees.

3. Something _____human is less than human.

Criss Cross

FILL IN the grid by answering the clues with keywords.

HINT: You'll want to add a prefix or suffix to a word in the clue.

ACROSS

2. The most strange
3. Someone who drives
7. Under the soil
9. Fill again
10. To exist before
11. The wrong match

DOWN

1. Full of fear
4. Full of help
5. Read wrong
6. Lacking power
8. More brave than

✓ Check It!

Page 63

Criss Cross

Across	Down
2. strangest	1. fearful
3. driver	4. helpful
7. subsoil	5. misread
9. refill	6. powerless
10. preexist	8. braver
11. mismatch	

Page 64

Grid Lock

1. sub • nor • mal
2. sharp • en • er
3. pen • ni • less
4. wealth • i • est
5. un • kind • ness
6. pre • teen
7. re • spect • ful
8. screw • driv • er
9. trou • ble • mak • er
10. re • pos • sess • ing
11. thought • ful • ness

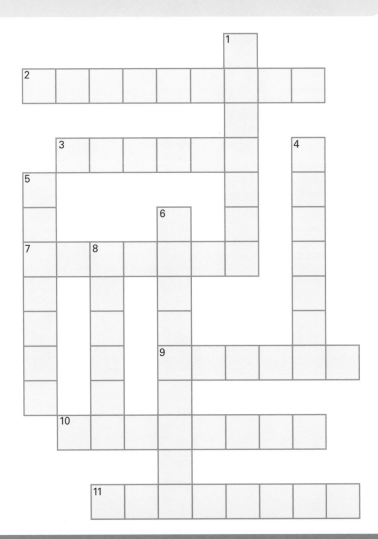

Grid Lock

FILL IN the grid with these words, writing one letter in each box starting from the left. Be sure to put each word in a row of the right length.

screwdriver	preteen	sharpener
wealthiest	unkindness	repossessing
subnormal	troublemaker	thoughtfulness
penniless	respectful	

HINT: Pay close attention to where the syllable dots are in the row.

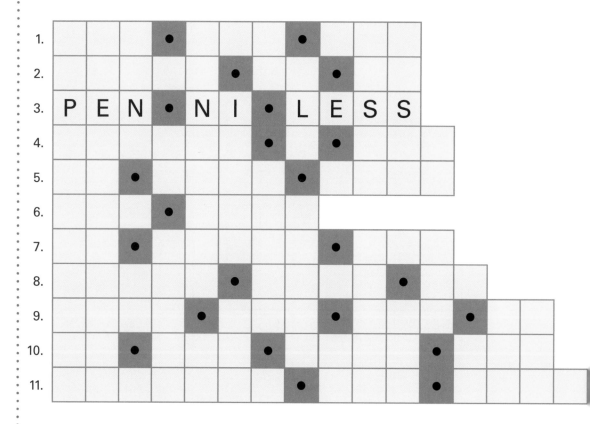

Keywords

When the letter "a" says its name, that's the long **a** sound, as in *hey* or *play* or *cake*. But hey! The word *hey* doesn't even have the letter "a" in it! Yep. The long **a** sound can be spelled lots of different ways.

READ the paragraph. The words in **bold** are your keywords.

During the winter **holiday**, my family went on a **sleigh** ride. There were **eight** of us, including our **neighbors**. We must have **weighed** a ton, but the horses flew **straight** down the **trail**, **spraying** snow with their hooves. They only needed a short **break** each hour. After the ride, we went out for a **steak** dinner. What a **great** day. I can't **wait** to do it again.

FILL IN the blanks with the **bold** words in alphabetical order.

1. _____

2. _____

3. _____

4. _____

5. _____

6. _____

7. _____

8. _____

9. _____

10. _____

11. _____

12. _____

✓ Check It!

Page 65

Keywords

1. break
2. eight
3. great
4. holiday
5. neighbors
6. sleigh
7. spraying
8. steak
9. straight
10. trail
11. wait
12. weighed

Page 66

Stack Up

Long A Spelled "AY"
1. holiday
2. spraying

Long A Spelled "AI"
1. straight
2. trait
3. wait

Long A Spelled "EA"
1. break
2. great
3. steak

Long A Spelled "EIGH"
1. eight
2. neighbors
3. sleigh
4. weighed

Page 67

Blank Out!

1. straight
2. neighbors
3. weighed
4. eight
5. steak
6. spraying

Write It Right!

1. afr *a i* d
2. cr *a y* on
3. str *a* ngers
4. Th *e y*
5. aw *a* ke
6. gr *a y* / tod *a y*
7. ob *e y*

Page 68

Grid Lock

1. lo • cat • ed
2. cam • paign
3. break • down
4. re • ap • pear
5. sky • rock • et
6. straight • er
7. pre • ar • range
8. neigh • bor • ly

Stack Up

READ the keywords out loud. SORT them by how the long **a** sound is spelled.

break	eight	great	holiday
neighbors	sleigh	spraying	steak
straight	trail	wait	weighed

Long A, Spelled "AY"
Example: play

1. _____

2. _____

Long A, Spelled "EA"
Example: wear

1. _____

2. _____

3. _____

Long A, Spelled "AI"
Example: sail

1. _____

2. _____

3. _____

Long A, Spelled "EIGH"
Example: neigh

1. _____

2. _____

3. _____

4. _____

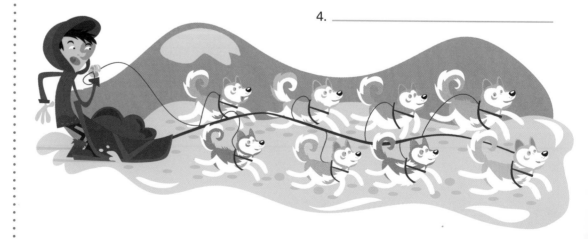

Blank Out!

FILL IN the blanks with keywords.

1. The band marched in a _____ line.

2. Our next-door _____ are moving away.

3. Uncle Troy wishes he _____ less.

4. Kyle built a computer when he was _____ years old.

5. Rare _____ is too gross to eat. Make mine well done!

6. Nick and I had a water fight while _____ the lawn. I won.

Write It Right!

FILL IN the missing letters to make the long **a** sound in each word.

Example: pl __a__ __y__

1. Don't be afr ____ ____ d.

2. I need a red cr ____ ____ on.

3. You shouldn't talk to str ____ ngers.

4. Ask the teachers. Th ____ ____ should know.

5. Are you aw ____ ke?

6. The sky is gr ____ ____ tod ____ ____ .

7. A dog must ob ____ ____ its owner.

Grid Lock

Remember, no matter how many letters it takes to make a vowel sound, they usually stick together in one syllable, unless the double vowels come from a prefix, like in *preexist* or *reexamine*.

FILL IN the grid with these words, writing one letter in each box starting from the left. Be sure to put each word in a row of the right length.

| breakdown | reappear | campaign | neighborly |
| skyrocket | straighter | located | prearrange |

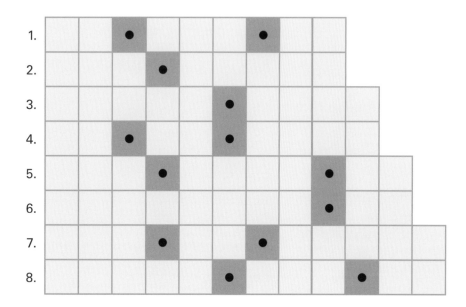

Keywords

There's more than meets the "i" in words like *high* and *dry*!
READ the paragraph. The words in **bold** are your keywords.

I was too **polite** to **deny** Great Aunt Ruby when she **invited** me to stay. Luckily one night seemed to **satisfy** her. She led me to the room I was to **occupy overnight**. The **firelight** made the shadows **multiply** into dozens of moving creatures. Suddenly I thought I saw a **slight** figure shimmering at my bedside! I began to sing a **lullaby**, then a nursery **rhyme** to calm myself down. When I turned on the light, there was nothing there. What a **fright**!

FILL IN the blanks with the **bold** words in alphabetical order.

1. _____   7. _____

2. _____   8. _____

3. _____   9. _____

4. _____   10. _____

5. _____   11. _____

6. _____   12. _____

✓ Check It!

Page 69
Keywords

1. deny
2. firelight
3. fright
4. invited
5. lullaby
6. multiply
7. occupy
8. overnight
9. polite
10. rhyme
11. satisfy
12. slight

Page 70
Stack Up

Long I Spelled "I-consonant-E"	Long I Spelled "Y"
1. invited	1. deny
2. polite	2. lullaby
	3. multiply
Long I Spelled "IGH"	4. occupy
1. firelight	5. rhyme
2. fright	6. satisfy
3. overnight	
4. slight	

Page 71
Criss Cross

Across	Down
2. rhyme	1. deny
4. lullaby	3. multiply
5. satisfy	
6. occupy	

Spell Check

1. airtight	4. fright
2. might	5. slight
3. delighted	6. eyesight

Page 72
Grid Lock

1. hair • style	5. mul • ti • ply
2. im • po • lite	6. oc • cu • py
3. de • ny	7. in • vit • ed
4. mag • ni • fy	8. po • lite

Bonus:

	+ "ed"	+ "ing"
1.	magnified	magnifying
2.	multiplied	multiplying
3.	satisfied	satisfying
4.	terrified	terrifying

Stack Up

READ the keywords out loud. SORT them by how the long **i** sound is spelled.

deny	firelight	fright	invited
lullaby	multiply	occupy	overnight
polite	rhyme	satisfy	slight

Long I, Spelled "I-consonant-E"
Example: kite

1. _____

2. _____

Long I, Spelled "Y"
Example: try

1. _____

2. _____

3. _____

4. _____

5. _____

6. _____

Long I, Spelled "IGH"
Example: tight

1. _____

2. _____

3. _____

4. _____

Criss Cross

FILL IN the grid by answering the clues with keywords.

ACROSS

2. A pair of words that sound alike

4. A sleepy song

5. Fulfill or please

6. Take up space, live in

DOWN

1. Turn down or refuse

3. Make more (like 6 x 2)

Spell Check

READ each sentence. CIRCLE the word that is misspelled. FILL IN the blanks with those misspelled words. Spell them right!

An astronaut's helmet must be airtite.

Jared myte join us, but he's not sure.

Mom was delited by her gift.

That big bug gave me a frite!

There is a slyte chance of showers.

I wear glasses to improve my eyesite.

1. _____

2. _____

3. _____

4. _____

5. _____

6. _____

Grid Lock

FILL IN the grid with these long **i** words, writing one letter in each box starting from the left. Be sure the dots properly break the words into syllables.

HINT: "-fy" is a suffix, so it's a separate syllable.

polite	occupy	invited	multiply
magnify	deny	hairstyle	impolite

1.
2.
3.
4.
5.
6.
7.
8.

Bonus

ADD the verb endings to these verbs:

Example: cry, cried, crying

Verb	Verb + "-ed"	Verb + "-ing"
magnify	1. _____	_____
multiply	2. _____	_____
satisfy	3. _____	_____
terrify	4. _____	_____

Keywords

Long **u** sounds like **oo**, but it's not always spelled that way.

READ the paragraph. The words in **bold** are your keywords.

I'm in a weird mood. At breakfast, I couldn't **choose** between **grapefruit** or orange **juice**. This **afternoon**, I **threw** my homework in the sink by accident. I went to the mall with a **coupon** for shoes. It was a good **value**: ten dollars off. I met a **group** of friends from school. I had no **clue** they'd be there. We went to the food court and **moved** all the chairs to one side. I came home two hours late with shampoo instead of new shoes. Mom didn't **approve**. She says I have a **screw** loose!

FILL IN the blanks with the **bold** words in alphabetical order.

1. _____   7. _____

2. _____   8. _____

3. _____   9. _____

4. _____   10. _____

5. _____   11. _____

6. _____   12. _____

Bonus

CIRCLE the other words in the paragraph that have a long **u** sound.

Stack Up

READ the keywords out loud. SORT them by how the long **u** sound is spelled.

afternoon   approve   choose   clue

coupon   grapefruit   group   juice

moved   screw   threw   value

Long U, Spelled "OO"
Example: soon

1. _____

2. _____

Long U, Spelled "OU"
Example: soup

1. _____

2. _____

Long U, Spelled "UE"
Example: due

1. _____

2. _____

Long U, Spelled "EW"
Example: chew

1. _____

2. _____

Long U, Spelled "UI"
Example: suit

1. _____

2. _____

Long U, Spelled "O"
Example: prove

1. _____

2. _____

Word Search

Oo-la-la! REWRITE the misspelled words, using the correct vowel(s) instead of "oo."
CIRCLE the words in the word grid. Words go down and across, not diagonally or backwards.

Example: noo, new

s**oo**per	1. _____
fr**oo**t	2. _____
st**oo**dent	3. _____
cr**oo**	4. _____
tr**oo**	5. _____
st**oo**	6. _____
bl**oo**berry	7. _____
sh**oo**maker	8. _____
y**oo**th	9. _____
n**oo**spaper	10. _____

```
S  H  O  E  M  A  K  E  R  I
U  B  L  U  E  B  E  R  R  Y
P  O  S  T  U  D  E  N  T  O
E  U  C  O  U  L  X  T  A  U
R  F  R  U  I  T  Q  R  R  T
W  O  E  S  T  E  W  U  L  H
N  E  W  S  P  A  P  E  R  P
```

Spotlight on "Yoo-hoo!"

When the letter "u" says its name, it's usually spelled with a "u." REWRITE the words, replacing "yoo" with "u" to spell the word right.

HINT: Watch carefully for the "e" at the end of some words.

ed**yoo**cate	1. _____
ab**yoo**se	2. _____
arg**yoo**e	3. _____
f**yoo**me	4. _____
h**yoo**man	5. _____
mis**yoo**se	6. _____
yoos**yoo**al	7. _____
bea**yoo**tiful	8. _____
contin**yoo**e	9. _____
aven**yoo**e	10. _____
f**yoo**el	11. _____
mon**yoo**ment	12. _____
porc**yoo**pine	13. _____
ref**yoo**se	14. _____

Keywords

"E" is a really popular vowel. It gets lots of help from its friends. At the end of a word, the long **e** sound is usually made by "y" or "ey," like in *happy* and *donkey*. Inside a word, "e" gets help from "a" and "i" too, like in *neat* and *chief*.

READ the paragraph. The words in **bold** are your keywords.

Now that I'm a **teenager**, I have the weirdest dreams. They're a real **mystery** to me. **Actually**, the other night, I dreamed that a **monkey**, a **turkey**, and a **weasel** were hiding in my **chimney**. These **creatures** were **thieves**, coming to steal the plants out of our **greenhouse**. In my sleep, I didn't have the **energy** to stop them. My knees were weak, and I couldn't speak. Finally, I woke up. Can you **believe** it?

FILL IN the blanks with the **bold** words in alphabetical order.

1. _____   7. _____

2. _____   8. _____

3. _____   9. _____

4. _____   10. _____

5. _____   11. _____

6. _____   12. _____

Bonus

CIRCLE the other words in the paragraph that have a long **e** sound.

✓ **Check It!**

Page 77

Keywords

1. actually	7. monkey
2. believe	8. mystery
3. chimney	9. teenager
4. creatures	10. thieves
5. energy	11. turkey
6. greenhouse	12. weasel

Bonus:

weirdest	sleep
dreams	knees
real	weak
dreamed	speak
these	finally
steal	

Page 78

Stack Up

Long E Spelled "Y"
1. energy
2. actually
3. mystery

Long E Spelled "EY"
1. chimney
2. monkey
3. turkey

Long E Spelled "EE"
1. teenager
2. greenhouse

Long E Spelled "EA"
1. creatures
2. weasel

Long E Spelled "IE"
1. believe
2. thieves

Page 79

Write It Right!

1. bel **i e** ve	6. f **e a** ture
2. Monk **e y** s	7. chimn **e y**
3. t **e e** nager	8. myster **y**
4. energ **y**	9. th **i e** f
5. ch **i e** f	10. pl **e a** se

Split It!

1. en•er•gy	6. li•brar•y
2. green•house	7. loy•al•ty
3. chim•ney	8. mem•o•ry
4. crea•ture	9. mys•ter•y
5. lib•er•ty	10. teen•ag•er

Stack Up

READ the keywords out loud. SORT them by how the long **e** sound is spelled.

actually	creatures	monkey	thieves
believe	energy	mystery	turkey
chimney	greenhouse	teenager	weasel

Long E, Spelled "Y"
Example: happy

1. _____
2. _____
3. _____

Long E, Spelled "EY"
Example: key

1. _____
2. _____
3. _____

Long E, Spelled "EE"
Example: meet

1. _____
2. _____

Long E, Spelled "EA"
Example: weak

1. _____
2. _____

Long E, Spelled "IE"
Example: retrieve

1. _____
2. _____

Write It Right!

FILL IN the missing letters to make the long **e** sound in each word.

Example: s __e__ __a__

1. I don't bel ____ ____ ve in ghosts!

2. Monk ____ ____ s live in the jungle.

3. My sister can't wait to be a t ____ ____ nager.

4. Turn off the lights to save energ ____.

5. Ty's dad is the ch ____ ____ f of police.

6. People say my nose is my best f ____ ____ ture.

7. Clean the chimn ____ ____ before having a fire in the fireplace.

8. I love to read a good myster ____ novel!

9. That squirrel is a th ____ ____ f! He stole my hot dog!

10. Always say "pl ____ ____ se" and "thank you."

Split It!

SPLIT the keywords into syllables, using dots to mark the breaks.

Example: oodles   oo•dles

energy	1. _____	library	6. _____
greenhouse	2. _____	loyalty	7. _____
chimney	3. _____	memory	8. _____
creature	4. _____	mystery	9. _____
liberty	5. _____	teenager	10. _____

Spotlight on Plurals Again

Did you notice something weird about the words *monkeys* and *turkeys*? They're not spelled *monkies* and *turkies*. That's because when a word ends in "ey," you usually just add an "s" to make it plural. FILL IN the blanks with the plural of each word.

HINT: Check the ends of the words carefully.

Example: key   keys

Singular	**Plural**
monkey	1. _____
liberty	2. _____
knee	3. _____
chimney	4. _____
army	5. _____
library	6. _____
flea	7. _____
donkey	8. _____
jockey	9. _____
memory	10. _____
bumblebee	11. _____
journey	12. _____
mystery	13. _____
energy	14. _____
valley	15. _____

Word Search

FILL IN the blanks by solving the clues. CIRCLE the answers in the word grid. Words go down and across, not diagonally or backwards.

HINT: Remember to look for prefixes and suffixes.

Plural of **mystery**   1. _____

Past tense of **occupy**   2. _____

Plural of **ox**   3. _____

Adverb of **slight**   4. _____

Plural of **valley**   5. _____

Improve + "-ing"   6. _____

Plural of **flea**   7. _____

Lacking **value**   8. _____

One who **multiplies**   9. _____

Plural of **lullaby**   10. _____

M	U	L	T	I	P	L	I	E	R
O	C	C	U	P	I	E	D	A	F
V	A	L	L	E	Y	S	L	N	L
I	M	P	R	O	V	I	N	G	E
M	Y	S	T	E	R	I	E	S	A
O	N	E	T	B	R	S	O	L	S
X	S	L	I	G	H	T	L	Y	E
E	L	U	L	L	A	B	I	E	S
N	V	A	L	U	E	L	E	S	S

Spell Check

READ each sentence. CIRCLE the word that's misspelled. FILL IN the blanks with those misspelled words. Spell them right!

1. Come over hear and say that!   _____

2. What a beeyootiful necklace.   _____

3. I haven't seen Teena in ate days.   _____

4. Let's not argyoo about it.   _____

5. I can't wait for the party tonite!   _____

6. The stars are really brite in the sky.   _____

7. The last car on the train is the cabuse.   _____

8. Tariq ways himself on the scale.   _____

9. Don't moove! There's a bee in your hair.   _____

10. I want to introdyooce you to my friend.   _____

11. Our car had a brakedown yesterday.   _____

12. Everyone needs a good edyoocation.   _____

13. Do you hear the baby's heartbeet?   _____

14. Tyoolips are my favorite flower.   _____

15. That poem doesn't even rime.   _____

16. Olive has a great sense of stile.   _____

17. My brother just joined the militaree.   _____

Keywords

Remember the Oodles? Well, now let's meet their cousins, the Oodels and the Oodals.

READ the paragraph. The words in **bold** are your keywords.

When I went to the **hospital** to get my tonsils out, everyone was **gentle** and treated me like a **royal** visitor. I shared a **double** room with another kid and put my **personal** stuff in a **metal** locker. I wore a warm **flannel** bathrobe, slippers all day, and an ID bracelet with my name on the **label**. I got get-well cards from my class and the school **principal**. And my parents brought me almost a **barrel** of ice cream! I wrote all about it in my **journal**. The nurses called me a **model** patient, but I was very glad to go home!

FILL IN the blanks with the **bold** words in alphabetical order.

1. _____
2. _____
3. _____
4. _____
5. _____
6. _____
7. _____
8. _____
9. _____
10. _____
11. _____
12. _____

Stack Up

READ the keywords out loud. SORT them into the categories.

> barrel   double   flannel   gentle   hospital   journal
>
> label   metal   model   personal   principal   royal

Oodles
Example: tickle

1. _____

2. _____

Oodals
Example: medal

1. _____

2. _____

3. _____

4. _____

5. _____

6. _____

Oodels
Example: level

1. _____

2. _____

3. _____

4. _____

Criss Cross

FILL IN the grid by answering the clues with keywords.

ACROSS

1. A tag inside your clothes
4. A diary where you write your thoughts
5. Like a king, queen, or princess
6. A place filled with doctors

DOWN

2. A container for pickles, wine, or monkeys
3. A soft, warm fabric

Mix & Match

In each box, MATCH a syllable on the left with a syllable on the right to make a word. DRAW a line between the two syllables to match them. REWRITE the words you matched in the blanks.

an	el	1. _____
lev	al	2. _____
wea	el	3. _____
trem	sel	4. _____
med	ble	5. _____
vow	gel	6. _____

crys	nel	7. _____
o	nal	8. _____
ped	tal	9. _____
fi	val	10. _____
tun	tel	11. _____
ho	al	12. _____

Oodles and Oodels (and Oodals)

Word Blocks

FILL IN the word blocks with words of the same shape from the list.

| angel | angle | barrel | brittle | label |
| ladle | general | personal | principal | principle |

1.

2.

3.

4.

5.

6.

7.

8.

9.

10.

Keywords

No, you're not going crazy. Sometimes there are letters in words that you just don't hear. Three common silent letters are "k," "t," and "w."

READ the paragraph. The words in **bold** are your keywords.

I'm **writing** a story about a **knight**. One day, someone **knocked** on the door of his **castle**. It was an old lady asking for help. The knight refused to **listen**. The lady got on her **knees** and begged, but he slammed the door in her **wrinkled** face. The next day, the knight found a silk thread **knotted** around his fingers. He couldn't **unwrap** it, or even cut it with a **knife** or a **sword**. Now I need to write how he finds the **answer** to his problem. Got any ideas?

FILL IN the blanks with the **bold** words in alphabetical order.

1. _____
2. _____
3. _____
4. _____
5. _____
6. _____
7. _____
8. _____
9. _____
10. _____
11. _____
12. _____

Stack Up

READ the keywords out loud. SORT them by their silent letters.

answer	castle	knees	knife
knight	knocked	knotted	listen
sword	wrinkled	writing	unwrap

"W" Is Silent
Example: wrong

1. _____
2. _____
3. _____
4. _____
5. _____

"K" Is Silent
Example: know

1. _____
2. _____
3. _____
4. _____
5. _____

"T" Is Silent
Example: often

1. _____
2. _____

Spell Check

READ each sentence. CIRCLE the word that is misspelled. FILL IN the blanks with those misspelled words. Spell them right!

1. My shirt is very rinkled. _____

2. I wish I lived in a fairy cassle. _____

3. Jerome is good at riting stories. _____

4. Oh no! My shoelace is notted up. _____

5. We can't wait to unrap our gifts. _____

6. What's the anser to that question? _____

7. I nocked twice, but nobody was home. _____

8. Why doesn't anybody lissen to me? _____

9. My little sister has scabby nees. _____

10. A good knight always carries a sord. _____

11. Try cutting your meat with a nife. _____

12. My piano teacher hates rong notes. _____

13. I offen wonder if Shanice likes her new school. _____

Spotlight on Silent Letters

There are silent letters in many words. The easiest way to spot them is to look at the word, and then say it out loud. Give it a try! READ the sentences out loud. CIRCLE the silent letters in the **bold** words.

HINT: All the silents are consonants. Some words have two.

Example: I tied a knot in the string.

1. The kittens **nestled** near their mother.
2. I caught **two** fish today!
3. Did you **climb** that tree?
4. Coach is blowing his **whistle**.
5. Can't you read the **sign**?
6. It's time to **rhyme**.
7. You look like you've seen a **ghost**.
8. **Autumn** is my favorite season of the year.
9. We spent a week on a tropical **island**.
10. Oh! I got a paper cut on my **thumb**.
11. My Uncle Barry **wrestles** alligators.
12. Muriel ate the **whole** pie by herself.
13. The mama cow is feeding her **calf**.
14. You'll find a **wrench** in the toolbox.
15. Grandma **knitted** an ugly sweater for me.
16. I use lotion to **soften** my hands.

Keywords

The letter "n" sounds nice when it's on its own, but when it teams up with "k," it sounds a bit different.

READ the paragraph. The words in **bold** are your keywords.

On Mom's birthday, Dad gave her a bracelet of gold **links sprinkled** with diamonds that **twinkled** in the light. But Mom **ranks** number one in losing jewelry. She once dropped an emerald ring at the ice **rink**, snagged and broke an earring on her **pink** coat, and lost her favorite jade **monkey** necklace in the **trunk** of the car. Before you could **blink** your eyes, the birthday bracelet fell in the **sink**. She should keep her stuff at the **bank**! Next year, Dad's getting her nothing but **junk**, so it's okay if she loses it.

FILL IN the blanks with the **bold** words in alphabetical order.

1. _____
2. _____
3. _____
4. _____
5. _____
6. _____

7. _____
8. _____
9. _____
10. _____
11. _____
12. _____

✓ Check It!

Page 91
Keywords

1. bank
2. blink
3. junk
4. links
5. monkey
6. pink
7. ranks
8. rink
9. sink
10. sprinkled
11. trunk
12. twinkled

Page 92
Stack Up

Rhymes with *Think*	Rhymes with *Chunky*
1. blink	1. monkey
2. links	
3. pink	**Rhymes with** Tank
4. rink	1. bank
5. sink	2. ranks

Rhymes with *Hunk*	Rhymes with *Wrinkled*
1. junk	1. sprinkled
2. trunk	2. twinkled

Page 93
Add It Up

1. wink
2. stink
3. blink
4. sink
5. drank

6. tank
7. chunk
8. drink
9. rank
10. prank

Bonus:
1. skunk
2. flunk
3. blank
4. yank

5. sank
6. honk
7. wrinkle

Page 94
Word Blocks

1. blanket
2. monkey
3. chunky
4. drinking
5. shrinking
6. thankful
7. wrinkle
8. sprinkle

Stack Up

READ the keywords out loud. SORT them by rhyme. FILL IN the blanks with the sorted words

| bank | blink | junk | links | pink | monkey |
| ranks | rink | sink | sprinkled | trunk | twinkled |

Rhymes with *Think(s)*
Example: wink

1. _____

2. _____

3. _____

4. _____

5. _____

Rhymes with *Tank(s)*
Example: blank

1. _____

2. _____

Rhymes with *Wrinkled*
Example: crinkled

1. _____

2. _____

Rhymes with *Hunk*
Example: sunk

1. _____

2. _____

Rhymes with *Chunky*
Example: spunky

1. _____

Add It Up

ADD or SUBTRACT the **bold** letter somewhere in the word to make a new word. FILL IN the blanks with the new words.

Example: fat + l = flat,   smart − s = mart

ink	+	w	=	1. _____
ink	+	st	=	2. _____
link	+	b	=	3. _____
stink	−	t	=	4. _____
rank	+	d	=	5. _____
thank	−	h	=	6. _____
hunk	+	c	=	7. _____
rink	+	d	=	8. _____
crank	−	c	=	9. _____
rank	+	p	=	10. _____

Bonus

You'll have to rearrange the letters to figure out these tricky ones!

sunk	+	k	=	1. _____
funk	+	l	=	2. _____
bank	+	l	=	3. _____
(bank − b)	+	y	=	4. _____
(sink − i)	+	a	=	5. _____
(hunk − u)	+	o	=	6. _____
(twinkle − t)	+	r	=	7. _____

Word Blocks

FILL IN the word blocks with words of the same shape from the list.

| wrinkle | thankful | blanket | sprinkle |
| chunky | monkey | drinking | shrinking |

1.

2.

3.

4.

5.

6.

7.

8.

Keywords

Sometimes, the letter "f" needs a break and brings in his friends "ph" and "gh" to do his work for him.

READ the paragraph. The words in **bold** are your keywords.

My friend Frank and I are working on a **graphic** novel, like a comic book. First it was about a **tough elephant** who falls in love with an **orphan dolphin**. But then we decided to make it about a **gopher** who's teaching his **nephew** the **alphabet**. When we talk on the **telephone**, Frank **laughs** so hard he starts to **cough**. Then his mom says we've had **enough** fun. Frank's a great friend!

FILL IN the blanks with the **bold** words in alphabetical order.

1. _____ 7. _____
2. _____ 8. _____
3. _____ 9. _____
4. _____ 10. _____
5. _____ 11. _____
6. _____ 12. _____

✓ **Check It!**

Page 95
Keywords
1. alphabet
2. cough
3. dolphin
4. elephant
5. enough
6. gopher
7. graphic
8. laughs
9. nephew
10. orphan
11. telephone
12. tough

Page 96
Write It Right!
1. alphabet
2. cough
3. dolphin
4. elephant
5. enough
6. gopher
7. graphic
8. laughs
9. nephew
10. orphan
11. telephone
12. tough

Page 97
Criss Cross

Across
2. orphan
3. telephone
5. nephew
6. graphic

Down
1. gopher
4. elephant

Split It!
1. e•nough
2. phan•tom
3. el•e•phant
4. proph•et
5. neph•ew
6. go•pher
7. dol•phin
8. laugh•ter
9. rough•ly
10. cough•ing
11. al•pha•bet
12. pheas•ant

✓ Check It!

Page 98

Spotlight on Silent "GH"

1. knight
2. caught
3. neighbors
4. fought
5. naughty
6. frighten
7. daughter
8. bought
9. taught
10. eight
11. stoplight
12. through
13. midnight

Write It Right!

REWRITE the misspelled keywords, using "ph" or "gh" instead of "f."

Example: rouf   *rough*

alfabet	1. _____
couf	2. _____
dolfin	3. _____
elefant	4. _____
enouf	5. _____
gofer	6. _____
grafic	7. _____
lafs	8. _____
nefew	9. _____
orfan	10. _____
telefone	11. _____
touf	12. _____

Criss Cross

FILL IN the grid by answering the clues with keywords.

ACROSS

2. A child with no parents

3. What you use to call your friends

5. The son of your sister or brother

6. Using pictures instead of words

DOWN

1. A small animal like a squirrel

4. Animal with a long trunk

Split It!

SPLIT these words into syllables, using dots to mark the breaks.

HINT: READ each word out loud. LISTEN to the vowel in the first syllable.

Example: asleep   a•sleep

enough	1. _____	dolphin	7. _____
phantom	2. _____	laughter	8. _____
elephant	3. _____	roughly	9. _____
prophet	4. _____	coughing	10. _____
nephew	5. _____	alphabet	11. _____
gopher	6. _____	pheasant	12. _____

Spotlight on Silent "GH"

Most of the time, when you see "gh" in a word, you don't pronounce it at all. That's because it's helping the vowel. READ each sentence. CIRCLE the word that's missing a "gh." Then FILL IN the blank with the word. Put the "gh" back!

HINT: Check the ends of the words carefully.

Example: Turn out the (lit) and go to bed.   _light_

He is a knit in shining armor.

Jamal caut the first fish.

The Patels are good neibors.

Ron and I fout about chores last week

Lissa was punished for being nauty.

Did that spider friten you?

Julio and his wife have a baby dauter.

Yesterday, Maria bout a new coat.

Greg taut me how to ride a bike.

There will be eit people at dinner.

There's a stoplit at that corner.

You can't drive throu that way.

On New Year's Eve, I stay up until midnit.

1. _____
2. _____
3. _____
4. _____
5. _____
6. _____
7. _____
8. _____
9. _____
10. _____
11. _____
12. _____
13. _____

Write It Right!

FILL IN the blanks with the missing letters of each word.

Example: I can't w_a_it to go to Florida!

1. After practice, I go str ____ ____ ____ ____ t to my room.

2. My old bathing s ____ ____ t is so small, it's

    skint ____ ____ ____ t!

3. I started lifting w ____ ____ ____ ____ ts to get strong.

4. We drove through a tunn ____ ____ in the mountain.

5. Our car had a br ____ ____ kdown on the

    h ____ ____ ____ way.

6. All of the army officers report to the gener ____ ____ .

7. My parents really like our n ____ ____ ____ ____ borhood.

8. Can you unscr ____ ____ the cap of the shamp ____ ____ ?

9. Little Gina is learning the al ____ ____ abet.

10. The smoke from the fire went up the chimn ____ ____ .

11. I have a c ____ ____ pon for five cents off a candy bar.

12. Dad puts lots of sugar on his grapefr ____ ____ t.

13. I get doub ____ ____ my allowance if I make dinner

    every night.

14. On Sundays, Mom puts my hair in br ____ ____ ds.

Stack Up

READ the words out loud. SORT them into these categories.
FILL IN the blanks with the sorted words.

unwrapped	library	thumb	terrify
refuel	mystery	preoccupy	sandcastle
memory	knocking	multiply	clueless
bluebells	dragonfly	busybody	untrue

Long I, Sound Spelled "Y"

1. _____

2. _____

3. _____

4. _____

Long U, Sound Spelled "UE"

1. _____

2. _____

3. _____

4. _____

Long E, Sound Spelled "Y"

1. _____

2. _____

3. _____

4. _____

Has a Silent Letter

1. _____

2. _____

3. _____

4. _____

Keywords

Some words, like *asleep*, aren't pronounced the way they're spelled. The "a" in *asleep* is not pronounced like an "a" because it isn't stressed. Instead, the "a" in *asleep* sounds like **uh**.

READ the paragraph. The words in **bold** are your keywords.

> All **seven** of us went to the zoo. After we **arrived**, we **divided** into groups. My group went to see the **parrots** first. My brother's group headed straight for the **zebras** and lions. Mom went **alone** to the snakes **because** nobody else **appreciates** snakes. Eventually we **abandoned** the animals and ate **salads** for lunch. On the way home, we were **delayed** by traffic, so we all **pretended** to be our favorite animals to pass the time. What a great day!

FILL IN the blanks with the **bold** words in alphabetical order.

1. _____
2. _____
3. _____
4. _____
5. _____
6. _____

7. _____
8. _____
9. _____
10. _____
11. _____
12. _____

Write It Right!

REWRITE the misspelled keywords, using the correct vowel instead of "uh."

Example: uhsleep   asleep

sal**uh**ds

b**uh**cause

sev**uh**n

uhbandoned

zebr**uh**s

uhrrived

d**uh**layed

uhlone

parr**uh**ts

uhppreciates

d**uh**vided

pr**uh**tended

1. _____

2. _____

3. _____

4. _____

5. _____

6. _____

7. _____

8. _____

9. _____

10. _____

11. _____

12. _____

Blank Out!

FILL IN the blanks with keywords. CIRCLE the letter in each word that sounds like **uh**.

1. Our package _____ late but undamaged.

2. The stray puppy had been _____ by its owners.

3. Aunt Miriam's flight was _____ by bad weather.

4. Dad gets mad because nobody _____ his cooking.

5. We always _____ our holiday candy into three piles.

Write It Right Again!

REWRITE these misspelled words, using the correct vowel instead of "uh."

Example: happuhly   happily

uhfficial	1. _____
uhdopt	2. _____
uhlarm	3. _____
uhbserve	4. _____
uhpparent	5. _____
uhthority	6. _____
b**uh**fore	7. _____
uhvoid	8. _____
b**uh**neath	9. _____
b**uh**wilder	10. _____
beaut**uh**ful	11. _____
plent**uh**ful	12. _____

Spotlight on UH-gain

There are lots of words that start with **uh**. Can you spot them?

CIRCLE the word in each sentence that starts with the **uh** sound.

Example: I can't believe he did it (again!)

1. Will you accompany me on the piano?

2. We're building a new addition onto our house.

3. The judge announced the winners.

4. Is arithmetic the same thing as math?

5. Ronnie likes to arrange the flowers for the table.

6. I warned Celine that she'd be arrested for stealing!

7. Mr. Ling took me aside to tell me my painting was great.

8. Dad assured me that we would still go to the game.

9. The alligator attacked the men in the boat.

10. Are you even aware that I'm here?

11. Your birthday is a special occasion.

12. Tell me your opinion on football versus baseball.

13. The original recipe used butter, but Mom changed it.

14. Come on up to my apartment for dinner.

15. When spots appeared on my face, I knew I had chicken pox.

Keywords

Life is short. Who's got time for whole words? Instead of writing *I am*, we write *I'm*. And instead of saying *you will*, we say *you'll*, right? Words combined like that are called CONTRACTIONS. READ the paragraph. The words in **bold** are your keywords.

I'm sure **you've** heard it all before, but **here's** the problem: Mom will go into my room, and **she'll** start screaming because **there's** some stuff on the floor. It **isn't** the end of the world! **We've** been through this again and again. I **would've** cleaned my room, but I **don't** have the time. Mom just **doesn't** get it. I say, **let's** agree to disagree, **that's** all.

FILL IN the blanks with the **bold** words in alphabetical order.

1. _____
2. _____
3. _____
4. _____
5. _____
6. _____

7. _____
8. _____
9. _____
10. _____
11. _____
12. _____

Add It Up

FILL IN the blanks with the keyword that "solves the problem."

Example: I + am = I'm

there	+ is	=	1.	
you	+ have	=	2.	
here	+ is	=	3.	
we	+ have	=	4.	
does	+ not	=	5.	
is	+ not	=	6.	
she	+ will	=	7.	
let	+ us	=	8.	
that	+ is	=	9.	
would	+ have	=	10.	
do	+ not	=	11.	

DON'T feed the bears!

Add It Up Again!

FILL IN the blanks with the contraction that "solves the problem."

HINT: The underlined letters get dropped.

Example: you + <u>ha</u>ve = you've

are	+	n<u>o</u>t	=
did	+	n<u>o</u>t	=
have	+	n<u>o</u>t	=
would	+	n<u>o</u>t	=
should	+	n<u>o</u>t	=
where	+	<u>i</u>s	=
they	+	<u>a</u>re	=
he	+	<u>i</u>s	=
he	+	<u>wi</u>ll	=
we	+	<u>ha</u>ve	=

1. _____

2. _____

3. _____

4. _____

5. _____

6. _____

7. _____

8. _____

9. _____

10. _____

Pick the One!

Every contraction has this: '. It's called an APOSTROPHE, and it goes where the dropped letter used to be. CIRCLE the contraction that has the apostrophe in the right place.

Example: theyr'e (they're)

1. shouldn't   should'nt

2. was'nt   wasn't

3. does'nt   doesn't

4. haven't   have'nt

5. ther'es   there's

6. you've   youv'e

7. aren't   are'nt

8. could'nt   couldn't

Word Blocks

FILL IN the word blocks with words of the same shape from the list.

HINT: Watch for the apostrophes!

| aren't | didn't | doesn't | she'll |
| they're | what's | would've | you've |

1.

5.

2.

6.

3.

7.

4.

8.

Keywords

Maybe the trickiest thing about spelling is that some words sound the same but are spelled differently. These words are called HOMOPHONES. Words like *write* and *right*, or *hear* and *here* are tricky. But not too tricky for YOU!

READ the paragraph. The words in **bold** are your keywords.

My older sister Theresa once tried to bake a **pear** tart. She did **not** do anything **right**! She was supposed to **pour** stuff into a bowl and **beat** it together, but it seemed like she just **threw flour** all over. When it was time to **break** the eggs, she dropped them instead. The **whole** kitchen was a mess. I **knew** mom **would** be mad for a **week**, so I helped Theresa clean up. She owes me one!

FILL IN the blanks with the **bold** words in alphabetical order.

1. _____
2. _____
3. _____
4. _____
5. _____
6. _____
7. _____
8. _____
9. _____
10. _____
11. _____
12. _____

Blank Out!

FILL IN the blanks with the keyword that sounds like each word.

pair

weak

flower

write

beet

new

wood

knot

hole

brake

through

poor

1. _____

2. _____

3. _____

4. _____

5. _____

6. _____

7. _____

8. _____

9. _____

10. _____

11. _____

12. _____

Spell Check

READ each sentence. CIRCLE the homophone that's wrong. *Write* the *right* homophone in the blank.

We burn would in our fireplace.

I love my knew video game!

Pour Joey lost his favorite jacket.

Luis got a cool pear of shoes.

We need a brake after all that work.

Aunt Sherri wants to right a novel.

Is your birthday next weak?

The chipmunk ran into a whole.

That flour smells so nice.

That is knot true at all.

Ick! I can't stand beat salad!

Did you here that sound?

Now wear did I put that towel?

I put it over they're.

Grace got every answer write.

1. _____

2. _____

3. _____

4. _____

5. _____

6. _____

7. _____

8. _____

9. _____

10. _____

11. _____

12. _____

13. _____

14. _____

15. _____

Blank Out!

FILL IN the blanks with the right homophones.

through/threw	1. Abby _____ a ball _____ the window.
bee/be	2. If Dora was stung by a _____ , she would _____ sick.
blue/blew	3. We _____ bubbles until we were _____ in the face.
planes/plains	4. People fly in _____ over the Midwestern _____.
tail/ tale	5. Mrs. Park tells a great _____ about a rat who lost its _____.
some/sum	6. _____ kids can't stand to do a _____ on the board.
stair/stare	7. I felt everyone _____ at me as I stood on the top _____.
weather/whether	8. Did they say _____ the _____ would be good?
there /they're	9. Hurry! I think _____ already _____.
there/their	10. The Jackson's new car is over _____, by _____house.
hour/our	11. If we wait an _____, we can have _____ usual table.
so/sew	12. You _____ clothes _____ nicely!
high/hi	13. _____ there! Do you go to my _____ school?
way/weigh	14. What's the best _____ to _____ an elephant?
two/too	15. You _____ girls are much _____ sleepy to stay up.
paws/pause	16. The dogs _____ to lick their _____.

Keywords

Congratulations, you've spelled a lot of words! But there are always more. And some are really tough. Are you ready for a challenge?

READ the paragraph. The words in **bold** are your keywords.

Our neighbor, Ms. Cordero, has a smart family. Her son is a **scientist** who does **experiments** with **amphibians**, like frogs and **tortoises**. She has two **nieces** that play in a professional soccer **league**, but they're on **separate** teams. You would probably **recognize** her daughter, who's a famous actress. And her husband makes great cakes for special **occasions**! As for Ms. Cordero, she runs a company that **manufactures** MP3 players. Compared to the Corderos, my family seems lame. But that's not our **fault**. When you're around the Corderos, you're **surrounded** by geniuses!

FILL IN the blanks with the **bold** words in alphabetical order.

1. _____

2. _____

3. _____

4. _____

5. _____

6. _____

7. _____

8. _____

9. _____

10. _____

11. _____

12. _____

✓ Check It!

Page 113
Keywords

1. amphibians
2. experiments
3. fault
4. league
5. manufactures
6. nieces
7. occasions
8. recognize
9. scientist
10. separate
11. surrounded
12. tortoises

Page 114
Split It!

1. au•thor•i•ty
2. a•rith•me•tic
3. an•nounce
4. ac•com•pa•ny
5. ex•per•i•ment
6. man•u•fac•ture
7. oc•ca•sion
8. rec•og•nize
9. sci•en•tist
10. sep•a•rate
11. sur•round
12. tor•toise

Page 115
Criss Cross

Across
3. scientist
4. manufactures
6. surrounded
7. separate

Down
1. occasions
2. nieces
5. recognize

Word Challenge

✓ Check It!

Page 116

Stack Up

Words with Doubles
1. bul•le•tin
2. hip•po•pot•a•mus
3. im•me•di•ate•ly
4. op•po•site
5. suf•fi•cient
6. im•pos•si•ble

Words with No Doubles
1. bal•ance
2. ben•e•fit
3. col•o•ny
4. lin•en
5. op•er•a•tion
6. sal•a•man•der

Split It!

SPLIT these words into syllables, using dots to mark the breaks.

authority	1. _____
arithmetic	2. _____
announce	3. _____
accompany	4. _____
experiment	5. _____
manufacture	6. _____
occasion	7. _____
recognize	8. _____
scientist	9. _____
separate	10. _____
surround	11. _____
tortoise	12. _____

114

Criss Cross

FILL IN the grid by answering the clues with keywords.

ACROSS

3. Someone who knows a lot about plants or chemicals

4. Builds in a factory

6. Enclosed on all sides

7. Disconnected, not shared

DOWN

1. Events or celebrations

2. Your brother's daughters are your ___.

5. To know by sight

Stack Up

Time for a flashback. Remember syllables and double consonants? If a syllable has a short vowel sound, it probably ends in a consonant. And you usually split a double consonant between the double letters.

SORT these words by doubles and no doubles.
SPLIT the words into syllables, using dots to mark the breaks.

balance	benefit	bulletin	colony
hippopotamus	immediately	linen	opposite
operation	salamander	sufficient	impossible

Words with Doubles

Example: op•por•tu•ni•ty

1. _____
2. _____
3. _____
4. _____
5. _____
6. _____

Words with No Doubles

Example: mel•on

1. _____
2. _____
3. _____
4. _____
5. _____
6. _____

Word Blocks

FILL IN the word blocks with words of the same shape from the list.

HINT: Watch for the apostrophes!

brightly	couldn't	endless	miscount
prepaid	recycle	subtotal	swiftness
their	they're	unhappy	wasn't

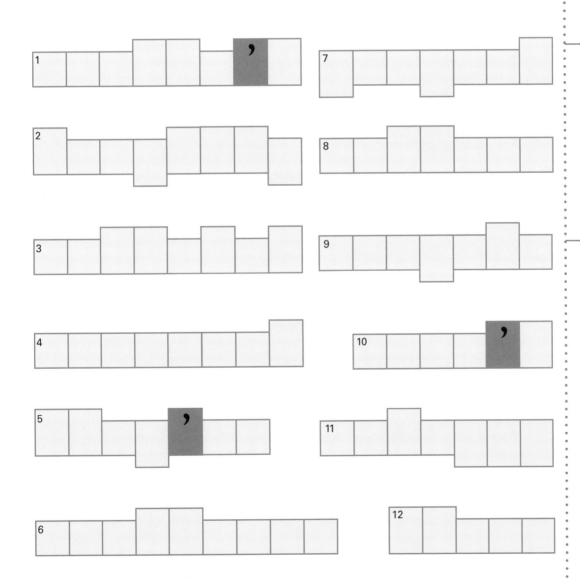

Spell Check

READ each sentence. CIRCLE the word that's misspelled. FILL IN the blanks with those misspelled words. Spell them right!

Brynne will be a syentist some day.

1. _____

It was the hotist day of the year.

2. _____

Mom told us to settuhl down.

3. _____

Terence needed three stichiz in his arm.

4. _____

No one will recuhgnyze you in that mask.

5. _____

The air was filled with butterflys.

6. _____

Yoo've got a pimple on your nose.

7. _____

We went shoping at the mall.

8. _____

I don't know why you're smileing.

9. _____

Mom always says to ask politeley.

10. _____

The hints are very helpfull.

11. _____

The box says to preeheat the oven.

12. _____

Travel through time? That's imposible!

13. _____

My dog is good at catching mouses.

14. _____

Amy's not her daughter, she's her knees.

15. _____

You are as slow as a tortuss.

16. _____

Woulden't you like to know?

17. _____

abandoned
actually
afternoon
alone
alphabet
amphibians
answer
answers
appreciates
approve
arrived
babies
backyard
bank
barefoot
barrel
baseball
basket
beat
because
begged
believe
birthday
blink
bodies
boils
break
bridle
bunches
calmer
calves
candle
careless
carry
castle
cattle
chicken

children
chimney
choose
churches
cities
clapped
cleaner
closely
closer
cloudless
clue
communities
companies
completely
cooks
costume
cough
countries
coupon
creatures
cupcake
darkness
delayed
delightful
deny
divided
doesn't
dolphin
don't
double
eight
elephant
energy
enough
experiments
fabric
factories

families
fault
fearless
fields
final
finally
finest
firelight
flannel
flopped
flour
flowers
follow
football
foxes
fright
geese
gentle
gentler
gopher
grabbed
grandmother
grapefruit
graphic
grateful
great
greenhouse
greets
grills
gripped
group
handful
handle
happiest
happily
here's
heroes

hikes
holiday
holler
hooves
hospital
hugging
hurry
I'm
inches
invited
isn't
journal
joyful
juice
junk
kitten
knees
knew
knife
knight
knocked
knotted
label
lady
largest
laughs
league
let's
links
listen
lives
loaves
longer
lullaby
lunches
mainly
manufactures

melt
men
metal
mice
middle
misbehave
misinformed
misleading
model
monkey
moved
multiply
mystery
neatest
needle
neighbors
nephew
nicer
nieces
not
occasions
occupy
oldest
orphan
outside
overnight
oxen
parrots
pear
perfectly
personal
pillow
pink
pinned
planning
play
plentiful

Spelling Words Index

polite
popcorn
pour
precaution
preschool
preteen
pretended
principal
program
properties
puddle
purest
purple
questions
quicker
quickly
quietest
ranks
rapidly
rebuild
recognize
remind
repaint
review
rhyme
ribbon
right
rink
ripest
ripped
rodeo
rotten
royal
saddle
sadly
safe

salads
satisfy
scatter
scientist
screaming
screw
separate
seven
shallow
she'll
shyness
simple
sink
skies
skipping
sleigh
slight
slowly
smarter
smell
soccer
sometimes
spraying
sprinkled
stable
starred
steak
stopping
stories
straight
strangely
strangest
stronger
students
successful
sunset

sunshine
super
surrounded
sword
table
talk
taller
teenager
teeth
telephone
territories
that's
there's
thieves
thimble
threw
tiger
title
tortoises
totally
tough
trail
trunk
turkey
twinkled
uncommon
unexpected
unlucky
unwrap
value
velvet
wait
want
weasel
week
weighed

we've
whole
widest
wildest
winter
wives
wolves
wonderful
worry
would
would've
wrinkled
writing
you've
youngest
zebras